CAMP 165 WATTEN

CAMP 165 WATTEN

Scotland's Most Secretive Prisoner of War Camp

VALERIE CAMPBELL

Whittles Publishing

Published by
Whittles Publishing,
Dunbeath,
Caithness KW6 6EY,
Scotland, UK
www.whittlespublishing.com

© 2008 Valerie Campbell
ISBN 978-1904445-60-9
Reprinted 2008
Reprinted 2009

Printed and bound in Great Britain
by 4edge Ltd., Hockley.

In memory of my parents
David Hunter Forsyth
1917–2005
and Margaret Sinclair
1939–2004

Contents

Acknowledgements

Without the help of numerous people and organisations, this book would not have been possible and the history of *Lager* 165 would have remained unwritten. For me personally this has been a tremendous journey and I would like to thank the following for all their assistance and encouragement with this project: Mr Whittle at the Ministry of Defence, Daniel Palmieri at The International Committee of the Red Cross, *The Scotsman* Newspapers, the Imperial War Museum, Alexander Braun at Panstwowe Muzeum Stutthof, Alan Hendry of the *John O'Groat Journal*, Michael Leventhal at Greenhill Books, John Thurso, Margaret Thurso, Maggie Harrison, Sandy Sutherland, Robert Miller, Alfred at the Brown Trout, David Sutherland, Mr and Mrs David McCarthy, Mr Spring at The History Centre, Surrey, Gilbert Gunn, Billy Miller, James Barnettson, Ronald Proctor, Thomas Smyth at the Regimental Headquarters of the Black Watch, Margaret Hammerton, Hector Sutherland, Margaret Booth, Mr and Mrs Geoffrey Leet, Mary Thompson, Joseph Ziegelbauer, Elisabeth Reeh, Evelyn Rosie, Betty Storm, George Henderson, Joan in Watten, Mr and Mrs Alan Harrold, Isabelle Thurley, Kathleen Hooker, Ingo Gunter d'Alquen, and George Watson. I thank of all the following for their help with publicity and support throughout the project: Laura Cumming, Morag and Bryan Anderson, Lorna and Richard McPartlan, Mrs Rhona Bain and her late husband Brian, Barbara and Andrew McElhinney, Morna and Mark Thomson, David Campbell, Danny and Karen Smith, Isabel Binnie, Sue Steven and Linsey Gullon. A special thank you goes to Herr Ludwig Schoon for answering all my questions on what camp life was like.

I would also like to thank Keith Whittles for believing in the book, David and Sandra Affleck and Eric and Christine Campbell for putting up with my endless talk on Camp 165 and reading the book in the early stages, and lastly my family, Douglas, Sam, Lauren and Kirsty for being there for me and helping me dig up our garden in Achingale Place. It is astonishing to think that so many of our neighbours in Watten are still living on the site of the camp. Robert Miller told me when he was young the area of Achingale Place was known as The Camps. Perhaps it will be known affectionately as that again by a new generation.

Foreword

In 1940 Wick suffered two bomb attacks by German aircraft. The first attack in Lower Pulteney caused the grievous loss of many children. The second, though casualties were far fewer, was disastrous for my father. Our house near the aerodrome was so seriously damaged that we were ordered to leave immediately and given temporary accommodation at the Station Hotel. Eventually my father found a house, and he moved to Watten several months later.

Life was fairly peaceful after the Wick bombings and my family gradually settled down to enjoy the community living in a small friendly village.

When we learned there was to be a prisoner of war camp in our midst, there were mixed feelings of apprehension, even fear. As the weeks passed into months though, without fearful incidents of dangerous prisoners roaming the countryside, villagers accepted the presence of the camp. As the book elaborates, in time some prisoners were allowed outside to work on neighbouring farms. Those who met and employed the prisoners found them harmless enough and acknowledged them as good and willing workers. But in truth we knew very little about the prisoners.

This was a story waiting to be told and who better to tell it than Valerie Campbell, the honours degree historian with Caithness connections. It is from *Camp 165 Watten* that we learn that all prisoners were carefully screened and only those of Class 'A' category were allowed out of the Camp. The garbled story we knew of a German escape was in fact the true story of several escapes which is now told accurately and in detail.

Little did we know that Camp 165 Watten was Britain's most secretive prisoner of war camp. Nor did we know that senior Nazi officers, some of them close to Hitler were imprisoned there. The life history of these men has been carefully researched and makes fascinating reading.

I knew both Lt.-Colonel 'Tishy' Murray and his junior officer, Captain Tim Gunn, well. Yet on the many occasions I met them, neither spoke of life in the camp. It was from the book that I learned both men had themselves been prisoners of war, a fact that had a bearing on the running of the camp.

Valerie Campbell told me that her interest in World War II came from her father's accounts of the war having been in North Africa with Montgomery and also seeing action in Sicily, Italy, France and Germany. How fortunate for us that she was inspired to write the history of Camp 165 Watten, which will remain part of the heritage of the village, but also an important piece of the wartime history of a camp in the North of Scotland – the most secretive prisoner of war camp in Britain.

Margaret Thurso

Introduction

The subject of prisoner of war camps in the United Kingdom is without doubt one of the major areas of war history that has not been investigated on a national scale. Some research has been underway on web sites and books mentioning camps scattered all over the United Kingdom, but in London at the National Archives in Kew, a wealth of material lies undisturbed. In my research for this book, I have found local people, former guards and prisoners feel that they are still bound by the Government promise they made over sixty years ago yet they want this history to be written. They were instructed not to talk or write of the camp in which the prisoners had been incarcerated. Slowly their reticence has lessened and many more people are now willing to speak of their experiences because they know that soon there will be no one left able to tell the tales of what happened during the time of the camp's existence. I hope this book will constitute a small piece of that secret history which will become part of a major study into prisoner of war camps in the United Kingdom.

Throughout World War II, prisoner of war camps sprang up on football pitches, race courses and estate grounds as well as on disused ground, or agricultural land commandeered by the Government from local farmers. The camp at Watten in Caithness was built on the latter by order of the Board of Agriculture in early 1943 and was to become Scotland's most secretive prisoner of war camp.

Every prisoner of war camp was allocated a number but there is a major problem with this, as the numbers do not run consecutively and there is a great deal of doubt that camps numbered over 1000 were in fact sequential. It is thought that around 490 camps actually existed. Some camps had duplicate numbers, which further confused the collection of information for historical researchers. At Watten, although the camp was numbered 165, initially it was a military training camp, with no known code or number; however it could be that when it became a prison camp it was indeed the 165th in the United Kingdom. Even through thorough investigation and gleaning what information is possible from local people about the time in question or sifting through newspapers or internet websites, building up a number sequence that is definitive may well prove to be impossible.

A fundamental question that has to be answered is what exactly a prisoner of war camp is. For this book, it is quite simply the place where captured German military personnel were incarcerated. These were not only ordinary foot soldiers of the Heer, submariners from the Kriegsmarine or members of the Luftwaffe but also members of the Waffen-SS. These men had been indoctrinated by Nazi policies and it was hoped that they would be reformed by showing them newsreels and re-educating them before their being sent back to post-war Germany. In some cases this proved difficult. British policy meant that Camp 165 closed its gates in early 1948 with the more hard line Nazis being transferred to stand trial or be interrogated elsewhere within Allied circles. Those deemed to be reformed characters were repatriated to their German homeland. Some of the hardliners were involved in the Nuremberg Trials, yet others escaped this fate. One of the more prominent men from Camp 165, a former concentration

Prisoners of Lager 165.

camp commandant, escaped between leaving Watten and being transported to an internment camp in Germany. He evaded recapture for several years, living a normal life, before being caught and sentenced for his part in the Third Reich's reign of terror. Not all the prisoners from Watten, or from the many other camps scattered around Britain, left. Indeed some stayed on in the locality, whether in Caithness, Perthshire or Yorkshire, marrying local girls and making a new life for themselves. However, some left a legacy behind them that they may have never have known about. In the 1940s, contraception was not so readily available as it is today. These blond-haired foreigners were charming and fresh-faced to the local girls, many of whom were entranced by their exoticism – as many attest today. Using charm, the prisoners managed to capture some sort of normality, no matter how short-lived, into their lives. This made life inside the camp bearable. Watten was classified as a base camp. It was a centre from which military activities were co-ordinated, including organisation and supply, but eventually it was seen as the place where the most zealous Nazi men should be sent, including, as mentioned earlier, members of the Waffen-SS, Hitler's elite fighting force. These included Gunter d'Alquen, the editor of the Nazi propaganda newspaper *Das Schwarze Korps,* and Paul Werner Hoppe, the second commandant of Stutthof concentration camp in Poland. Hitler's one-time adjutant Max Wünsche was also held at Watten, as was the famous U-boat captain Otto Kretschmer, the 'Wolf of the Atlantic'.

The camp was the most northerly on the United Kingdom mainland and if any of the men tried to escape there was nowhere for them to go. Some men did escape briefly from the compound but all of them were recaptured within days. Many of them simply gave themselves up when they were approached and were relieved to get back to the camp, for they had no idea what the surrounding area held for them. This area of Caithness is barren, flat and, in the main, inhospitable. Camp life seemed altogether the better option.

A number of camps fared much better with the passage of time than Watten. Some have been made into museums with re-enactments of what camp life may have been like. Others are run down but do show in their own dilapidated way that they existed. The last Nissen hut was dismantled at Camp 165 in the late 1990s to build a house on its site. A small number of huts have been recycled on local farms and crofts. A few concrete block buildings remain as testament to the camp, but without local knowledge they would simply be disused buildings. It is only thanks to a few people interested enough to look back at the past and be bold enough to tell their stories that a picture of camp life can be built up. A physical picture of the camp has only been possible thanks to local men and women who have copies of drawings and plans which allow a small piece of British history to be preserved.

A passer-by would have little idea about the rich history of Watten and its association with World War II. Most people associate the village with Alexander Bain, the inventor of the electric clock and fax machine in the 19th century, or its famous loch which is renowned for trout fishing. They would not know of its significance as a prisoner of war camp that held some of the most infamous men in the Nazi regime.

It is important that Camp 165's history should be told. It fills in gaps in the lives of some prominent prisoners and the links between camps presenting a rich tapestry of information. Within the following pages, the secrets of Camp 165 and its place in history will be revealed.

Chapter 1

Beginnings

———————

Watten is remote. It lies seven miles west of Wick on the banks of the loch with the same name, and it is precisely because of its isolation that the village was chosen to house a secluded military training camp in the early 1940s.

Caithness has a distinguished military history with several disused airfields scattered around, including Castletown on the north coast only twelve miles from Watten, and Skitten, roughly seven miles from the village. More importantly from a strategic point of view was Burifa Hill at Dunnet Head, which was used as an RAF monitoring station during World War II, covering the waters that led to Orkney and the United States of America beyond. It is known that the LORAN long wave navigation radar system was used here and the station was at the head of the northern chain. The largest building on site was the operations block, and there was a transformer house and three smaller buildings as well as a stand-by house. Two radars were operational here, the AMES Type 30 and a Type 57, and although it was demoted to caretaking duties after the war, it was still operational and kept a close eye on this approach route. Soldiers from the Watten camp worked here from 1943 until the end of hostilities, and later, prisoners of war were able to spend some time here. The antenna systems and old buildings are still in evidence.

The landscape in Caithness was invaluable for training and subsequently for holding captives. The military training could go on in secret and unperturbed and when the Watten camp changed to the prison camp, there was nowhere for the prisoners to go. The farmland surrounding the camp was flat with few hiding places, plus the terrain was foreign to them. The prisoners knew that if they were spotted, they would be hastily returned to camp to face punishment. Life in the camp may have been difficult but at least the men were fed and had a relatively dry place to put down their heads.

In the south, it was doubtful that anyone with the exception of the military hierarchy would have even known the camp at Watten existed as it was the most secretive of all the camps in Scotland. Other camps such as Camp 21 at Comrie, known as Cultybraggan, are well known. It held a number of Nazi prisoners similar to those held in the Far North and indeed, research has shown some of them were transported north to Watten.

Unlike Camp 165, Camp 21 still exists and is in a good state of repair. In fact it is the most intact of all the prisoner of war camps in the United Kingdom. The Nissen huts remain in very good condition, considering they were first erected in 1939 and the camp held many of the soldiers who fought as part of the Afrika Korps, known in Germany as the Deutsches Afrikakorps, during the North Africa campaign between 1941 and its surrender in 1943. It could hold up to 4000 prisoners, but it is likely to have held less than this at any one time. Figures for all the camps are only estimates for there was continual fluidity as men arrived, were classified into different sections, and sent on to other camps more appropriate to their new classification. Watten received some prisoners from here after this reclassification.

One of the most famous prisoners in the Perthshire camp is said to be Rudolph Hess, Hitler's deputy, although in all fairness, he was allegedly only incarcerated at Cultybraggan for one night after he was captured in Scotland following a crash landing on the night of 10 May 1941. His mission, he had claimed, was to speak to the Duke of Hamilton to thrash out a peace deal. He was sent to England the next day, remaining a prisoner of the British until he was returned to Germany in 1945 to stand trial at Nuremberg. According to Churchill, he was to be treated like any other high-ranking German prisoner, even though he was diagnosed by British military psychiatrists as being insane and only out for all he could gain for himself. At the International Military Tribunal he was sentenced to life imprisonment. He committed suicide in 1987 at Spandau at the age of 92.

Today, the camp, two miles south of Comrie, which was used as a training facility for a number of groups including the Territorial Army, has been sold by the MoD to the Comrie Community Trust. It is a fine example of what a prisoner of war camp looked like and Watten was built in the same manner.

The military training camp at Watten was completed on 27 August 1943 at a cost of just over £30,000. The men to be stationed there had to live with the local people until the camp was completed. Like many projects, it ran behind schedule, even though it was erected in a relatively short space of time. It was a village within a village. It had barracks for the soldiers to sleep in, a mess hall and canteen, a first aid post, a repair shed and armourer's shop, to mention but a few of the facilities. Some buildings are still in existence today, such as the rank-and-file quarters as well as the former water pump house, although the sleeping quarters have all but gone. None of these remaining buildings are in good condition. However, a few have been made into garages for local people.

In a survey carried out by the county architect Mr William Wilson a number of years after the camp had gone, the concrete bases of Nissen huts and other constructions were still in evidence. The plans show obvious signs that it had been greatly expanded from the 1943 plan of the army camp in the mainly Achingale Place area. Row upon row of concrete bases had been left. These bases formed the accommodation for hundreds of prisoners of war who arrived two years after its completion. It was originally extended to accommodate a Polish unit, although they were moved on when the war ended. The Polish troops had been relegated to tented accommodation by the Wick River, but they had been flooded out and sought refuge

2

in the camp. At this stage, local people were unsure where the Polish troops' loyalties lay. The uneasiness with these troops was something that was carried on after they had moved out of Watten and the war had long ended.

In 1943 officer quarters were built, as well as those for warrant officers and sergeants, and rank-and-file men, who greatly outstripped the other groups. The officers' and warrant officers' messes were completely separate and the rank-and-file had none. Behind the officers' mess were the ablutions and latrines for the officers, both of which were of the Nissen hut type. Not all the buildings were Nissen though. Some were built of concrete block, such as the latrines for warrant officers, sergeants, and the rank-and-file, for the military camp did not have the urgency of building as the prisoner of war camp was to have later. Other buildings were Ministry of Supply or Ministry of War Production type. For example, the garrison headquarters signal store and signal offices were of the Ministry of Supply type yet the garrison headquarter offices were from the Ministry of War Production.

The Ministry of War Production type huts were usually made from pre-cast reinforced concrete. Their sizes varied depending on their function. When the original camp was completed, only six of these were built which housed rank-and-file quarters and the garrison headquarter offices as mentioned above. Three buildings, electric light engine shed, the showers and drying room, and the warrant officers, sergeants and rank-and-file latrines, were built solely of concrete block. Concrete was used extensively in the construction of buildings, as it was thought they would last longer.

Nissen huts had been devised by a Canadian, Colonel Peter Nissen during World War I, as the need for the speedy construction of shelters was paramount in the theatre of war. Pre-World War I, living accommodation for soldiers abroad meant spending hours erecting shelters; however, the need for speedy shelters became more urgent during fighting in France in 1916. There were already shelters known as Armstrong sectional hutting type, but these were bulky and difficult to ship across the English Channel to the fighting men. A new design was required and, in May 1916, the first Nissen hut was inspected by the British at the Pays de Calais and deemed ideal. An order was made in August that year. Nissen claimed he designed the huts allegedly inspired from something he had seen at home in Canada and they were an instant success. The British government of the day ordered them in vast quantities to provide accommodation to the soldiers in the field. However, these early huts encountered problems and only after trial and error did a fairly flexible but rather standard design work, using iron bows and concrete end panels.

The huts in Watten generally measured thirty-six feet by sixteen wide and roughly eight feet high with windows at either side of the front and back doors. The curved corrugated iron roof was held in place by iron straps. According to 1943 plans, many of them were fastened together to make larger spaces, such as for dining. That was the beauty of them; they were flexible.

Inside, the space was lined, although it made no real difference to the temperature. In winter the huts were freezing and the iron roof shook in the violent winds. If the rain came down in torrents, the noise on the corrugated roofs prevented the men from catching much sleep. In the summer months, the huts became too warm and stuffy and often the nights were spent trying to cool down. The foundations on which many of the huts in Watten stood were concrete as they were assumed to be a fairly permanent feature, especially once the prisoners of war began to arrive. No one knew how long they would be incarcerated. These shelters took six men around four hours to construct. At the opening of the camp in 1943 around one hundred Nissen huts had been constructed.

A major problem with the huts was condensation. In the winter months, when temperatures outside reached −12°C, the heat inside created a massive amount of condensation that ran down the walls. The wet atmosphere in turn caused some of the men to become ill. Frequently, bedding became very damp and it was difficult to dry the sleeping bags and blankets, therefore common winter diseases easily took hold of the men. This problem of condensation remained unsolved and is perhaps why the attraction of the Nissen hut had already begun to dwindle by the beginning of World War II. Their decline in popularity was also due to the curved corrugated iron as it was rather awkward to transport. Yet, at Watten, and other camps in the United Kingdom, they were seen as the solution to housing so many of the prisoners due to their practicality in their quick and easy erection. The pre-existing huts from the military training camp were never going to be able to accommodate more bodies and building using concrete block would have taken so much longer.

Whether the buildings at Watten were Nissen, Ministry of Supply or Ministry of War Production type, they all had two things in common. They were quick to erect and they were cheap. Their sole purpose was temporary accommodation, although it was unclear how temporary they were to be.

The camp originally had to cater for the many different ranks. At its opening in 1943 here were forty-four officers, fifty-six warrant officers and sergeants and seven hundred and two rank-and-file men. Other members of staff allowed in the camp in its early days included ten NAAFI (the Navy, Army and Air Force Institutes) assistants with one manageress overseeing them. The NAAFI provided the British military personnel at the camp with their canteens and shops. They still provide this vital service today both at home and overseas. The NAAFI had two Nissen huts for food service and another one, which was extended, for staff quarters. Working under the difficult conditions that came with rationing, the women did well to put meals on the table, which were varied and nutritional. Much of the food was transported directly to the camp from further south rather than using up local supplies. On the menu were such delicacies as oatmeal soup, steak and potato pie, macaroni, and rhubarb crumble and vinegar cake. One of the most popular dishes at Watten was corned beef hash.

Five Nissen huts were given over to rank-and-file cookhouses on the eastern side of the camp with two blocks of two huts joined together to make up their dining areas. They did their own cooking, as the NAAFI catered for the officers, although the rank-and-file were able to purchase goods from the NAAFI shop.

Next to the NAAFI was a septic tank, which was built on site. However no plans were ever drawn up for it and it was not built along standard design lines. Yet it carried out its purpose with only a few minor hitches.

Originally on Banks Road, which leads from Watten down to the tiny hamlet of Mybster on the main A9 road, there was a complex array of buildings encased by primitive barbed wire

Some of the prisoners were allowed to swim in Loch Watten
during the summer months.

fencing. The remnants of this wire show signs that the wire barbs had been put on by hand, twisted by pliers. If that was indeed the case, it must have taken a long time for the fencing to be finished, for there were hundreds of yards of it encircling the whole camp when it became the prison camp. But at its inception, a few thin rows of wire encircled the buildings on Banks Road. These were the messing and grocery store, the main NAAFI staff quarters and the electric light engine shed. The largest of these was the engine shed. It housed the Crossley engine with a brake horsepower of twenty-five driving the generator that supplied the electricity to the camp. The engine shed was built of concrete block and was the largest building within the camp's ground.

The messing and grocery store were yet another two Nissen huts knocked together, and was later to become the focal point of prisoner of war Camp 165 – its theatre. Adapting these original buildings for later purposes was never a problem. When the deliveries came to Watten, the rank-and-file men unloaded the goods and with fine precision they stacked the food and other goods in the grocery store. Mainly, the food was tinned so it would keep for longer and the mice and rats would not be able to nibble their way through to it. Oatmeal and other cereals did however create problems, but traps were set and the cereals inspected on a daily basis to combat the problem.

The former police house in Achingale Place was the bread and meat store for the camp in 1943. Like most of the buildings, it was a Nissen hut, the concrete base of which is found in the plans of William Wilson, the county architect during the 1950s. Again, much of the meat was

The pump house, which supplied water to the camp, still stands at the fringe of the former site of Camp 165.

tinned, although some fresh meat was delivered. Bread was either the national loaf (a brown bread) or it was baked on site, depending on what was available.

Opposite the bread and meat store was the first aid post, where dressings, medicines and minor surgical equipment was kept. This was later moved and upgraded into an infirmary where some of the German prisoners, who had medical training, were able to practice. The limitations of the first aid post meant only minor ailments could be dealt with. The Dunbar Hospital in Thurso was the main port of call for more serious afflictions.

The water supply for the camp came from Loch Watten, via the pumping plant on the shore of the loch, which consisted of a natural gas and oil engine and had the capacity to pump at 7.4 brake horsepower driving the centrifugal pump to obtain fifty gallons per minute against the head of a hundred and twenty-five feet. The pump house near the camp itself was built from concrete block and can still be seen. It is perhaps important to note that the water pumped into the camp was also pumped back out. It is by sheer luck the water never caused deaths from the many different water-borne diseases such as dysentery or typhoid fever.

Dotted around the camp were galvanised iron sheet tanks to collect rainwater, but there was a problem with them. They tended to corrode and burst and their life expectancy was only ever a few years. Buckets and other water collectors were also used to gather rain, which many of the British soldiers preferred to the galvanised tank water.

In 1945, however, the camp's function changed. In May of that year, the first German prisoners of war arrived. They were transported on trucks and trains, having been captured on the Continent, mainly in Normandy during the Allied advances. Shipped over to the United Kingdom, they were unsure of their fate. Many of them were young conscripts of no more than seventeen or eighteen years and had grown up in the shadow of the Hitler Youth and the Third Reich's emphasis on German nationalism. These boys had heard tales from their childhood of how Germany had surrendered in 1918 yet that the soldiers of the day had wanted to fight on. That generation of disgruntled men had led to the rise of a Fascist power that Europe had not seen before. The bitter surrender fuelled nationalism and led to an age group utterly intent on destroying those who had betrayed and battered the Fatherland twenty years before. They were sure that the only way was by constructing a propaganda machine to instil in every child the desire to seek revenge. It was hugely successful as fathers told their post-war sons of how great Germany could become. The Wall Street Crash and the Depression that followed only helped these men further their cause for a Greater Germany. Hitler's oratory in the 1930s brought Germany the greatness it had been seeking for the best part of two decades. An economic recovery on a massive scale took place, as the unemployed joined the army, navy and air force, and those who did not join the military went into the factories to make armaments as Germany geared up for confrontation and its execution of the *Lebensraum*, or living space, policy.

Growing up with this burden, many of the young soldiers had been horrified at the devastation and destruction war could bring, and losing friends in the field only made things worse for the conscripts. They realised the brutality of war and many felt betrayed. Germany in the early 1940s had been on the brink of world domination only to be beaten back and destroyed by the Allies. Morale amongst the men was the lowest it could have ever been.

Yet others held in Watten over the three years when it was known as *Lager* 165 were notorious, both in Germany and in her neighbours and growing steadily within other Allied circles. Report upon report named men who had tortured not only foreign nationals, but their own, or who had held a great deal of power under the Hitler regime. Their capture was a devastating blow not only to those men themselves who had once held the power of the Nazi regime in their hands, but to the morale of the German people back home. Many had been highly decorated, some personally so by none other than Adolf Hitler himself and now they were incarcerated in a foreign land.

Apart from the conscripts, others held at Watten included SS-Oberführer Otto Baum, one of the most highly decorated soldiers of the Third Reich and commander of the 16th SS-Panzergrenadier-Division *Reichsführer SS* at the end of the war. Another was a member of the V2 rocket team, Dr Paul Schröder, who worked under Generalmajor Dr Walter Dornberger, whose pioneering work led to the development of the V2 rocket.

The prisoners destined for Watten were both the innocents caught up by Hitler's propaganda machine and the notorious for their fastidious belief in the Third Reich's place in the world and its domination of that world. When they were dropped off at the railway platform by the loch and marched up to the main camp, their lives were about to change.

Huts were rapidly erected by them in upper Achingale Place and in what is now part of the local football field to house these new internees. The bases of these were still visible many years after the huts themselves had been dismantled. Drawings by one of the prisoners in 1947, assumed to be Unteroffizier H. H. Walter, show the position of some of them. Although not part of the original camp, many of the new huts in the field became part of its history through their use as holding areas and are as integral in Watten's history as the remains of the old pump house or the other buildings dotted around the village.

During an inspection by the International Committee of the Red Cross (ICRC) one month after it became a prisoner of war camp, it was noted that the number of prisoners had already reached just over five hundred, including over seventy non-commissioned officers and four hundred and twenty men from the army, navy and air force. There were also a number of civilians. A small number of the prisoners had been born outside Germany but had German nationality and one of these could not speak a word of German, only Russian. At its height the camp held around 2800 prisoners, although it had the capacity for only 2000.

The number of huts at this stage in June 1945 which were habitable had reached seventy-seven. These included living quarters, dining facilities, reading room, a barber's and a detention hut. The camp infirmary was also under construction.

Construction of Camp 165 was ongoing for most of its lifetime. There never seemed a time when a new hut was not being built to accommodate the ever-increasing number of internees arriving daily. This was the case until late 1947, but as that year drew to a close, fewer men were being sent to Watten and more and more were either being sent to camps elsewhere in the United Kingdom or repatriated.

War camps in the United Kingdom were all but dismantled in the years following repatriation of most of the German soldiers in 1948. A few however do remain. One of the best known ones is in North Yorkshire at Malton. This was formerly Camp 83 and is now a dedicated museum. It gives a flavour of what camp life was like for the internees from World War II. Another, as mentioned, is Cultybraggan at Comrie, where the huts lie testament to the former role it played in wartime Britain.

When the German prisoners arrived at the camp in Watten they fitted in with the local community, with the exception perhaps of those deemed 'black', or more fanatical Nazis. Whether it was a conscious effort on either side is unknown but they were accepted as part of the war and post-war effort, and in the main, they caused no trouble. Accommodating as it was, the camp urgently needed upgrading by the time the first contingent of German nationals came in May 1945. Wear and tear of the original camp had taken its toll.

Chapter 2

Prisoner of War Camp 165

All over Britain, prisoner of war camps had been set up towards the last years of the war. Adolf Hitler already knew the war was lost by 1943 but he was unwilling to give up the fight and face the wrath of his people, so the fighting had continued. He buoyed them up with speeches, condemning the Allies and suggesting that victory was just around the corner. However, after the momentous events of June 1944 when the British, Canadian and American troops landed in Normandy, there was no getting away from the fact that Germany and her allies had been defeated. Still, the fighting soldiers kept going until their capture by the British and Canadian forces as they drove inland. These men were then shipped to Britain as prisoners of war.

In its early life as a prisoner of war camp, its commandant was Lt.-Col. P. H. Drake-Brockham. However, Drake-Brockham's time there was short-lived, for by November 1945, Lt.-Col. R. L. T. Murray from the Black Watch had taken over and he was there until the camp closed in 1948. Murray wrote about the camp for the *John O'Groat Journal*. He wrote that in the early days of the camp it consisted of one compound surrounded by wire and was under guard day and night by the sentries. There had been four observation towers built which were in each corner of the compound so the guards could keep watch over the prisoners. Towards the end of 1945 escorts for prisoners of war working outside the camp were removed as the prisoners were specially chosen because they were considered to be reliable in character.

In June 1945 each prisoner had received on arrival a sleeping bag and due to the climatic conditions, which were apparently very windy, two blankets. The number of blankets however increased later to three, no doubt because the men were more used to the warmer climes in their homeland, even in winter. Heating for the accommodation huts came from stoves and the lighting was electric, being carried over to the main camp from the Crossley engine in the engine shed on Banks Road. Five hundred and one men of the Heer, Marine, and Luftwaffe amongst others were incarcerated. Of these, there was only one officer, but seventy-one non-commissioned officers and 429 men. Their nationalities were German, by far the majority of the population, Austrian, Belgian and Polish, although the Poles numbered only two. Most of the prisoners had been captured since D-Day, 6 June 1944, and had been transferred from Camp 22, Pennylands at Auchenleck near Cumnock in Ayrshire. Like Watten, this camp had originally been taken over by the War Office to form a military training camp. The men billeted there were of many different nationalities, including the secretive members of the Free French who were being trained using SAS tactics. However, by the end of the war, it had been turned into a prisoner of war camp, housing at first Polish prisoners then German. Also, like Watten, the prisoners here, if deemed to be of suitable character, which in the main they were for the camp was not a special camp holding 'blacks', were allowed to go out of the camp compound and work on the local farms. Over half of the men transported to Watten in May 1945 were aged between thirty and forty and forty-one per cent were in the forty to fifty age group. Surprisingly, seven were aged over fifty.

The camp leader at this time was Wilhelm Macht, whose assistant was Oberführer Wilhelm Brinkenmeyer. On his acceptance as camp leader, Oberführer Macht had received papers on the conventions of the camp, to which prisoners were to adhere. These included discipline within the camp compound, the organisation of the camp, and behaviour outwith the camp if men were allowed out. Sanctions would be applied if prisoners did something that the Camp Commandant believed to be unfair, undisciplined or harmful. Other information included in the booklet was on food and clothing, the issuing of blankets, hygiene within the camp detailing bathing, hand washing and so on. Recreational activities, both mental and physical, religious practice and information regarding prisoners' mail, including parcels, was also incorporated into the booklet. Everything was clearly defined for the new internees.

Although the camp had already been established, more accommodation was being built at the time of the June ICRC inspection. The inmates were involved in the building of new huts. There were already Nissen huts and wooden huts, but the wooden ones were uninhabitable unless a lining was installed for the winter months. This was brought to the attention of the second-in-command at the camp, as Drake-Brockham was away on leave, so that something could be done about it. A large camp infirmary was also under construction at this time and the sanitary installations for the camp were in the process of being completed. For the time being though, pails had to be used. There were already hot and cold shower baths however, so at least the men could wash.

The infirmary was already in use even though it was incomplete. Central heating was up and running and all amenities had been installed. There were two wards, consisting of eleven beds. In the infirmary there was what were termed 'protected personnel'. These were members of the SS who posed the greatest threat to security and stability within the camp. In total there were nine men under this umbrella. Two were officers who were in the infirmary and the others were categorised as other ranks, five of whom joined the officers in the infirmary and two others who were held in the compound.

One thing mitigating their restricted life was being able to look forward to the ever increasing number of letters and parcels sent to the camp for them. May 1945 was the peak month, when one hundred and eighteen letters arrived from Germany and as many as twenty-eight parcels. Between March and July 1945, one hundred and ninety-one letters and thirty-

The recipient's prisoner of war number was a requirement of the parcel documentation to Camp 165 in 'Northschottland, ENGLAND'.

seven parcels were received from Germany. Parcels the men received contained cigarettes, which they could trade, sugar and dried fruits. Occasionally a huge treat of chocolates, or sweets, arrived. On the label there was a customs section in which the sender had to declare what was in the parcel and each parcel was weighed. Addressing the parcel, the sender also had to put the recipient's prisoner of war number, which was allocated to the men as they were processed.

By November 1945, the camp had changed dramatically. It had been divided up into Compound A and Compound B. Compound A held prisoners who were seen as no threat whatsoever. They were the ones who were trying to get on with their lives and were happy enough to pass their days without causing problems. Many of these men had been conscripts and had not wanted to fight on the frontline, but having been captured they felt safe in British hands, for if they had deserted whilst on duty in the field, they would have undoubtedly been shot. Compound B, for all that some in there were happy to bide their time in captivity, was far more complex. Many held in there were former members of the Hitler Youth and were seen as hard-line Nazis. Over three hundred and fifty men were in this compound alone.

DIE BUNTE BÜHNE.

One of a series of sketches assumed to be drawn by Unteroffizier H. H. Walter, a prisoner at Camp 165 Watten. The hut in this sketch is apparently where the theatre group rehearsed.

The total number of prisoners stood at almost one thousand three hundred. A break-down of the nationalities included nine hundred and twenty-nine Germans in Compound A, which was their grand total, and three hundred and forty-four in Compound B, with four Austrians, one Belgian and twenty-one Dutchmen. Of those in Compound A, three hundred and ninety-five were from the regular army, and included one hundred and ninety-seven from the SS, one hundred and seventy-nine from the Luftwaffe and one hundred and fifty from the German navy, the Kreigsmarine. There were also three customs men and two civilians. In Compound B, there were one hundred and sixty-six from the regular army, forty SS men, eighty-eight from the Luftwaffe and seventy-one from the navy. There was only one civilian held here along with four commercial servicemen, but all were staunch Hitlerite supporters and made no secret of it.

The original prisoners had been transferred and replaced by the others at the end of July and end of August. Amongst this new group were Luftwaffe pilots captured in 1940 and six prisoners from Canada. There were one hundred and forty-five buildings now within the camp. In Compound A, fifty-two buildings were used for accommodation purposes, with four used as canteens, two for kitchens and seven for latrines and showers. There were also eight used as workshops for the skilled craftsmen and one as a Protestant chapel. The compound leader was now Stabsoberfeldwebel Walter Lindner and his adjutant was Stabsfeldwebel Bruno Rokall, both of whom had been sent up from Camp 21 at Comrie.

Compound B, under the leadership of Hauptfeldwebel Hugo Fischer von Weikerstahl, had forty-two accommodation blocks, four buildings for latrines and showers, one for a canteen and others included one each for a laundry, an office, a quartermaster's store, a theatre, a Catholic chapel, although no Protestant chapel was available in this compound, and a classroom. Three buildings were used as bakeries. In both of these compounds, each man still received a sleeping bag with two blankets and it was promised that a third would be issued for the winter. They, like their earlier comrades, had been issued with clothing. Each man received three pairs of trousers and three shirts. Around a quarter of the men in Compound A and a tenth in Compound B still had their full German uniforms but they were well-worn. With winter fast approaching, the prisoners needed the new clothing, even if it was just to supplement the somewhat threadbare uniforms. Some put on the new clothes under their German uniform, as their symbolic gesture of defiance at being held in a military prisoner of war camp.

By November, the hospital was complete. In Barrack 1, there were two dormitories, consisting of fifty beds altogether, a bathroom, and toilets for the two members of the health care staff. Barrack 2 consisted of a kitchen, where the food was prepared solely for the invalids and the personnel looking after them. It also contained sanitary facilities. The doctors had separate barracks, which consisted of a surgical room, an office, two bedrooms for students learning under the doctor, a dental surgery and clinic. There was also a medical isolation hut and an accommodation hut for other students interested in medicine. Of these one was an officer and twelve students of other ranks. At that time, the infirmary was lucky in that there were two German dentists ready to help anyone in pain.

Requests made by the internees included study manuals for their courses, equipment for the theatre group such as clothes and make-up, song books and sheet music for the orchestra and, at the request of the Catholic chaplain, Hermann Müller, the small prayer book *Gebetbucher für Kriegsgefangend* published by the Vatican. The Protestant Chaplin, Oberleutnant Heinz Forster, asked for copies of the New Testament and hymn books. The medical officer, Stabsarzt Meinhard Keizl, put in a request for medical works and Swiss or German periodicals in order to stay updated with progress being made in the medical profession.

Each of the prisoners was consumed with the thought of the date of his repatriation. The war was over and they could not understand why they could not return home to their families and loved ones. It would be many months for some of these men. However the one thing that kept them going was the writing and receipt of letters. Although there were problems with mail getting to and from the Russian Zones in Germany, the prisoners wrote over nine hundred cards and letters to their loved ones from Compound A, with Compound B sending a lot less. However, the camp received mail for the men on a daily basis which was delivered by the ordinary Royal Mail postman. Compound A generally received more mail than Compound B.

Over the course of the next six months, the camp improved its accommodation. A number of the huts were tarred and other improvements made, such as the new flowerbeds and vegetable gardens to try and give it a homely feel. The huts had been tarred to help combat the severe weather experienced in the far north. Between October and April, snow and wind can be a huge problem therefore any improvements made proved beneficial over the winter.

A - LAGER · MITTELSTRASSE

Compound A's main thoroughfare.

By the early summer of 1946 the camp looked clean and tidy, and had been greatly improved. Some three hundred and eighty of the men had been transferred to other camps and others had arrived from as far afield as the United States of America, Canada once more and other camps within the United Kingdom. The type of prisoners had not changed, neither had their treatment, which was exactly the same as in other camps even if they were of a different character.

In May 1946, according to an article in the *John O'Groat Journal* written by Lt.-Col. Murray, a higher authority changed the status of the camp slightly. It was to be the chief CX camp, otherwise known as the chief Nazi camp. This was when it was split into two distinct compounds, different from the previous set up. Compound A was to house all non-CX types whereas B was to house the Nazi type. It was also at this time that the higher authority requested that the wire was removed from Compound A. Thus, the camp became partly a base camp (Compound B) and partly a working camp (Compound A). However, by November of that year, the camp was further split and now had three compounds. Compound A still held non-CX prisoners, and Compound B held the CX ones, but this new compound C held intermediaries. These were young men who although still considered Nazis were seen as

14

redeemable and it was thought it would be better to segregate them from those in Compound B who may have been a bad influence on them. As such, a more pronounced programme of de-Nazification was undertaken by the camp with these men.

The number of protected personnel stood at twelve in the infirmary, but in the compound, it had rocketed to eighty-six. In the infirmary, the senior medical officer, Keizl put in a request for all kinds of modern medical books to help him in his work.

By Christmas 1946, although there were fewer men in the camp, it still held over one thousand five hundred souls, mostly men from the Heer and Luftwaffe, with one hundred and sixty-two from the SS. For the first time, all of the prisoners were German. Of the one thousand five hundred and eleven prisoners, there were two officers and the rest of other ranks, forty-nine were classed as protected personnel. The set up had changed too. In Compound A, there were six hundred and forty-five men, but there were twelve at the hostel in Thurso, seven working with the Royal Air Force in Wick and thirty-four classed as billettees. These billettees were living at the farms on which they worked, and were trusted both by the military hierarchy and by the people who housed them. They had proved themselves to be no threat and were genuinely trying to make the best of their lives by helping the farmers and learning new skills. Many had never had the opportunity to work the land back home and they found it hard work but highly rewarding. The men in the camp were split thus: in Compound A, there were three hundred and sixty-six Heer (army), ninety-six from the Kriegsmarine, one hundred and forty from the Luftwaffe and ninety-one from the SS plus a few miscellaneous men. In Compound B, there was over a hundred more men incarcerated. These included four hundred and five from the German Army, one hundred and three from the navy, two hundred and twenty-three from the Luftwaffe and seventy-one from the SS. A railway worker was also held, as were four civilians.

The major change in the camp was to be found in Compound A where a special hut had been set apart for twelve non-commissioned officers whose movements had to be restricted for political reasons. Compound A was seen as a working camp, and B was reserved for 'black' prisoners of war although around four hundred of these men were allowed to work. These prisoners asked for more freedom but this was seen as impossible. Some from Compound B had been transferred to A and once again there had been changes with prisoners being transferred to other camps and new ones arriving, mainly from Canada. Around one hundred and twenty-five of the young prisoners were sent to the Youth Camp, Camp 180 in England, and seventy others had been granted repatriation status. Around sixty of the U-boat men had also gone to camps in England. Between May and December 1946 the camp reached its highest number of internees at two thousand eight hundred men. The camp struggled with this number, as its capacity, as already mentioned, was only two thousand. All available space was taken up with some men having to share a bed or sleep on the floors of the huts. Murray was unhappy about the situation and called for action to be taken to relieve the camp of some of its prisoners.

Another change in the camp was the escorted walks. The soldiers held in Compound A were allowed to go for walks unescorted. This was due in the main to a War Office blanket-order on all men categorised as 'A' prisoners. They were no longer any threat. Also the barbed wire surrounding that compound was taken down. Compound B was not so lucky. Their walks remained escorted and the wire stayed.

Because of the harsh winter weather endured by the men, it was noted that their underwear was inadequate, being too thin. It was after all late December. However, they wrapped up as best they could.

At Christmas the Protestants among the men were allowed to go to the services in Watten church, down near the loch on Station Road, both on Christmas Eve and Christmas morning. The men marched down to the Watten church on Christmas morning for the 10.30 service. The church was lit by oil lamps and a large Christmas tree had been beautifully decorated. The camp choir and orchestra sang and played during the service, which was attended by roughly 200 prisoners. The Scottish minister had welcomed the prisoners of war at the beginning of the service which was enjoyed by everyone who attended. Walter Freyer, one of the prisoners from the camp, played the church organ during the service. This must have been one of the most uplifting yet desperate times for the men. Christmas, in 1946, was not celebrated so much by the Scots as Hogmanay. New Year's Eve was the big celebration of the year. Yet these German soldiers brought a little part of German lore to the area. Celebrating Christmas was one of the major Christian festivals in Germany and they saw it as a very special time when trees were decorated and presents given in celebration of the birth of Christ. Yet, the festivities must have been tinged with sadness, for they were not with their loved ones back home, but in a foreign land with their freedom curtailed.

The Roman Catholic soldiers held their services in the camp's chapel. A Christmas Mass was held at 11.30 p.m. on Christmas Eve, conducted by the Roman Catholic chaplain, Hermann Müller, and another held at 8.45 on Christmas morning.

In the afternoon, at 3.30, a concert was held for Compound B in the dining hall of the compound, and later, another concert was held in the same venue for the men of Compound A. Music and song filled the air as the camp orchestra and choir played and sang traditional German Christmas songs. As they knew the words, the audiences joined in.

Letters and parcels had arrived in the run-up to Christmas. Although the system was by no means perfect, letters were getting through to the men from their families from the British, French, Russian and American zones in Germany. Difficulties had arisen in the summer when letters and packages were not getting through from Munich and Nuremberg but this seemed to have eased by December. Christmas cards arrived in huge quantities and the men used them to decorate their huts.

Eight months later, in August 1947, the number of men remaining at Camp 165 had dwindled to just over seven hundred and thirty, including sixteen officers and twenty men of other ranks who were protected personnel. There was also another Compound, labelled 'O'. This section of the camp was for officers only and was, like Compound B, surrounded by barbed wire. Compound A had been free of wire for almost a year. In this new compound were twenty-eight huts. Sixteen of them were accommodation, although some of these remained empty, two for kitchen and dining hall use and one each for latrines, ablutions and reading room. Others housed a hobby shop and canteen. The Camp leader of Compound O was SS Oberführer Harro Witt and his assistant was Oberstleutnant Ehrhardt Unger. The Compound held forty-three men of the Heer (or German Army), twenty from the Luftwaffe, twenty-one from the Marine and twenty-nine SS men. There was also one SS civilian and two members of the police force. The officers numbered one hundred and two with ten non-commissioned officers.

The political grading of prisoners at the camp had also changed. The categorisation of the men was scaled. Those who were of no threat were 'A' whereas those thought to be of some threat were 'B' and those who were of greatest threat to the United Kingdom security because of their strong beliefs in Nazism were either 'C' or 'C+'. The number of 'C' and 'C+' had been upgraded from Compounds A and B. New officers had arrived, categorised as 'C-', from other camps, including Camp 18, Featherstone Park in Northumberland, and Camp184, Llanmartin in Wales. As for non-commissioned officers in Compound B, there were approximately forty who still refused to work for the British authorities, so they remained in the compound, working willingly for the camp leader, Albert Liehsfeld, as they realised that by doing so they were benefiting their comrades.

Of the officers held in Compound O, Herzmark, the man responsible for screening them, graded fifty-five as 'C+'. Major Bieri of the Red Cross saw this as rather peculiar and he decided to bring it to the attention of the authorities concerned. He informed the London branch of the Red Cross of his concerns and left it to them to deal with. The reason for this was that this number was half of the men that Herzmark had screened. It seemed oddly high and as far as Bieri was concerned the issue had to be raised to find out the reason why. The authorities looked into this matter but the outcome is unknown.

August 1947 was part of a glorious summer in Caithness and this is reflected in the Red Cross report. Bieri wrote: 'This summer was the first which is really a "summer". Plenty of sunshine and warmth, both rather exceptional in that part of the North of Scotland'. A lot of outdoor work was taking place, such as repairs to the huts and vehicle maintenance, and some of the men from the camp were allowed to go down and swim in Loch Watten. Others, who either did not wish to go swimming, or were not allowed to, were able to sunbathe within the camp and work in the garden. The flowers were in full bloom giving the camp an attractive feel to it and morale was 'good as it can be in the circumstances'. Only a few individuals who resented their screening were unhappy. Those categorised as 'C+' were the most disgruntled of all the men, as they felt they had been in captivity for a long time and because they had greater restrictions placed upon them. An underlying anxiety was repatriation, especially in the officers' compound. They were classed as 'C' and after discharge to Germany did not know what would happen to them. It did not help them that letters from upgraded and other discharged comrades had arrived about the German local Labour Exchange methods, which were far from being positive. Unemployment back in Germany was high due to the demobilisation of troops and those who had been faithful to the Nazi cause were finding it ever more difficult to secure employment.

By January 1948 only a few months before the camp's closure, there were less than seven hundred men in the camp, including the detachment of one hundred men sent to the Orkney Islands to help with reconstruction. There were six hundred and eighty-nine Germans, two Austrians, one Argentinean and one Yugoslavian. Over all there were one hundred and four officers. The camp was no longer seen as a 'black' camp. Many of the men had been upgraded and transferred from Watten and it had very few new arrivals.

In his article, Murray wrote about the end of the life of the camp: 'In January 1948, more prisoners from Compound A were sent to other camps ... In February 1948, the remaining CX POWs were transferred *en bloc* to Germany. At the end of March the camp was closed, leaving only some two hundred prisoners to be transferred to other camps.'

Amongst most, the mood in the camp was buoyant, with the exception of the officers in Compound O, as long-awaited repatriation was underway. For the officers, what awaited them were de-Nazification courts on their return to their homeland. The new camp leader in O was the former editor of the German newspaper, *Das Schwarze Korps,* SS Obergruppenführer Gunter d'Alquen, as Witt had been moved on. Also amongst the other prisoners of note, last to leave were SS Hauptsturmführer Paul Werner Hoppe, the second commandant of Stutthof concentration camp, SS Oberführer Otto Baum, and SS Obersturmbannführer Max Wünsche, one-time adjutant to Adolf Hitler. Otto Kretschmer, the U-boat commander, had also left due to ill health.

Throughout all this time, Lt.-Col. Murray was praised for the way he ran the camp. In every Red Cross report the camp is complimented. It was seen as an excellent and very well run camp. Many of the prisoners of war, on the whole, felt satisfied with their treatment and considered the conditions as being good. In the August 1947 Red Cross account, even the prisoners told Bieri that they would not like to be transferred to any other camp. Bieri himself states that the camp treatment is 'absolutely correct ... and an excellent and well run camp'. Later Murray was praised by the prisoners too, who saw him as fair in the execution of his duties. In his own words, Murray wrote: 'There seems little doubt that the prisoners were contented at Watten, which was very largely due to the friendly attitude of the civilian popula-tion. [Murray had] received many letters from ex-POWs stressing this fact.' However, it was his over-riding influence that helped the camp gain such high praise.

In 1955 the praise heaped upon both the people of Caithness and on Lt.-Col. Murray was backed up by Herr Otto Lendemans, a former prisoner at *Lager* 165. As part of the summer programme of events organised by the Wick Civic Entertainment Committee, the male voice Kranzhoff Choir from Dortmund started off their Scottish tour there. Lendemans, a former Luftwaffe pilot, had been held at the prisoner of war camp at Watten and it was his wish, as leader of the choir, that the choir should start its tour in Caithness as a token of appreciation of the friendship and hospitality extended to prisoners during their incarceration at the camp.

The camp finally closed its gates in early April 1948 with the last prisoners being trans-ported south in late February on a special train, organised by the military, which left the station at Watten for an undisclosed destination, as the majority of the prisoners left at this point were hard-line Nazis incapable or unwilling to change. Some were to be handed over to war crimes investigators in Europe whilst others, the less hard-liners, were simply going back to a homeland that had totally changed from the one they had left in 1939. The military authorities, however, refused to comment on where the men were going.

Not all of the prisoners left Caithness however. Some of them were left behind to help with the handover. Others were becoming 'civilian' as Bieri put it. They had met local girls and intended to marry. The legacy of these men carries on to this day in the bloodlines created.

O – LAGER / ANTRETEPLATZ

The entrance to Compound O.

By the turn of the twenty-first century, little remained of Camp 165. Occasionally local people find artefacts, such as medicine bottles, drinks bottles, broken pottery or even tags with the name of the concrete manufacturer who had been used to lay the foundations of the Nissen huts. One tag had the following inscription: 'R.M.C. Heckmondwike 1940 No LB 250211.' This is a tiny find but an intricate part of the camp's history.

Occasionally rusted barbed wire that had surrounded the camp is found. One family found several metres of wire, some of it still in its original coil, testament to the changes in the treatment of the prisoners as the wire had either been ordered and never used, or it had been dismantled and rolled up when the prisoners posed no threat to the community.

These little pieces of physical history could have been lost in the Caithness landscape forever and historians may never have questioned their relevance.

Learning and Leisure

Even at its early stage of the camp life in June 1945, a theatre group and camp choir had sprung up. The theatre group consisted of fifteen members, and the choir had forty. The camp leader, Macht, requested an accordion and folk song books for the choir and plays for the theatre so they could put on productions to pass the time. A piano had already been provided for occasional use and they had two violins and home-made drums. This is one of the major success stories from the camp, for people from all over the county came to see these men perform and many years after the war had ended, members of the camp band returned to Wick to perform. Once every three weeks, the soldiers were shown a film and every Sunday, a newsreel was played to them. At all other times, the men could listen to the radio.

Among the activities available in June 1945, one that many of the men took up was learning a new language. English was the most popular with a class of one hundred and twenty-five pupils, but French and Czech was also taught. Arithmetic, shorthand and drawing were the other classes available, and when not studying, there was always the camp library with its three hundred books available. These books had been donated by local people, borrowed from the library in Wick or purchased out of the camp funds, but every one was checked for its suitability. The director of studies was Gefreiter Josef Brandhove, who took it upon himself to see these courses were available. He knew that by keeping the men occupied through learning and other activities, there should be no trouble, and that was indeed the case. Many of those who took up the classes were in the under twenty-five age group with a thirst for learning, and although some the older men tended not to show interest in such activities, there were no difficulties with them.

By November 1945 studies in the camp continued to increase. English, French, German conversation, Russian and Spanish were all being taught, along with modern history, geology, stenography and beekeeping. Numerous courses on architecture were being run from strategies of construction, woodwork, masonry and carpentry through to architectural design, land register work, and surveying. All of the courses were taught without the aid of any manuals, which is remarkable. English proved to be the most popular course, followed by accounting and commercial law. The directors of studies were Unteroffiziers Herbert Battermann and Alfred Radecker. Some of the prisoners from Compound B were allowed to mix with Compound

A men on the proviso they behaved and it was always at the discretion of the commandant. The camp still had a thriving theatre group of sixteen actors and the choir had around thirty members with an orchestra of sixteen musicians. The cinema screening had stopped for the moment and the camp awaited the arrival of a radio. The camp's other radio had gone with the previous prisoners to their new destination.

By the summer of 1946 even more recreational and study opportunities were available which remained important for their mental and physical well-being. By now four football teams had been formed from each compound and there were handball teams and boxing clubs. The prisoners from Compound B were taken out of the camp for a daily walk at around three in the afternoon. The band had proved over the years to be a great success. Originally, it had performed in the Watten village hall. The concerts were attended by the public from both Wick and Thurso and were increasingly popular. Because of its popularity, another venue was sought to accommodate the large numbers wishing to attend. The theatre group had expanded to 40 members and the theatre itself was complete. It was now very well equipped. There were also two choirs, one a church choir with between twenty and twenty-five members and a camp choir with between sixty to eighty people taking part. These arts were from that time onwards performed in the theatre so that as many people as possible could attend.

The number of books in the camp library had now reached over one thousand, including two hundred novels, as well as books on the subjects being taught, such as English and accounting. The radio was in use, and newsreels were still played, although there were still no films available to the men. Studies were continuing in both camps. Around five hundred men from Compound A and seven hundred from Compound B took part in the learning programmes available. The student leader, Hermann Mohrmann, was happy with the progress being made and with the books available to the prisoners, although no extra subjects were being taught. The books helped teaching and learning tremendously.

Classes from the new Compound O were held in August 1947 under the watchful gaze of Studienleiter Oberleutnant Alfred Pudelko and included learning English, which had a class of thirty, and remained the most popular of all the subjects taught. Botany was also now on offer, which four men took up. There was also plumbing, joinery and surveying. Their library had over seven hundred books, of which two hundred were fiction. However, SS Oberführer Harro Witt, the Compound O camp leader, made a request for more books, especially about handicrafts and hobby work, as well as more fiction and educational works. The men in this new compound, like the other two, were not to be deprived of learning new skills.

In Compounds A and B, the new subjects Russian, gardening and astronomy were available. Only five men studied Russian, but the gardening class had fourteen students and astronomy had thirteen. The study of astronomy was much enhanced as the black skies of Caithness provided an ideal backdrop for the observation of the stars and planets.

The theatre group was still thriving as was the camp orchestra. The theatrical group now consisted of thirty members and the orchestra of sixteen. The latter was considered to be excellent and both groups incorporated members from the whole camp. However, not everyone in the county of Caithness was happy with the orchestra.

Word had got round about the orchestra's popularity and at the town council's monthly meeting in Wick in July 1947, a debate took place to decide whether or not to invite the orchestra to Wick to give occasional concerts. The suggestion had been put forward by Bailie William Dunnet who told the meeting that a large number of music lovers had heard the band play at the camp but that there was insufficient seating for all those who wished to attend. However, inviting them to play in Wick would allow more members of the public to hear them as they played so well. Objections to the proposal was raised by Dean of Guild Alexander Miller, who objected on principle that they were indeed German prisoners, regardless of whether they were part of a good band or not. He suggested to the council members that it would be an insult to the men who had fought in the war against the German regime and that they should not be applauded in Wick. Bailie Dunnet's motion was seconded by Councillor Owen. Councillor Sutherland put forward a proposal that if the band was invited to play in the town by any of the local societies, then they should be allowed to do so. He moved an amendment that the proposals lie on the table. Voting was close at seven supporting the initial motion and seven supporting the amendment. Provost Sinclair, having the casting vote, decided to side with the amendment. There was to be no invitation for the band at that time. Feelings were running high. Had the band been allowed to play, there would always be the risk that some in the audience would cause a fracas and begin mocking the men, calling them Nazis and so on. On the other hand, it may have proved the best decision to allow them to play and allow people to see that they were ordinary men who had simply grown up and been nurtured in the shadow of a dictator. Wounds may have been healed, and a mutual understanding of each other may have been reached, but it was not to be, not at that time anyway.

The theatre group and the band were discontinued in January 1948. Sadly, as repatriation was in full swing, one of the band members was killed on his way home to Hamburg. The Glasgow to Euston, London express train was involved in a crash with a mail train in April 1948. On board was Werner Hans Kolln, an accomplished violinist who had been at Watten for nine months. Kolln had been a U-boat commander and had been captured with two other survivors from a fatally hit submarine, having managed to evade capture on the numerous other occasions when his boats were struck. During his time at Watten, he had been allowed to go out to visit a local farm at Stirkoke. A young boy had noticed him on the road as he cycled past and eventually asked about the violin case. Kolln played his violin for the family that lived at the farm for over three hours with the beautiful music filling the house. The tall German in his naval uniform was passionate about his music. According to reports, he had been intending to visit a friend in Bristol on his way back to Germany but he never made it. His mother had been eagerly awaiting his return when the news of his death arrived. He was among twenty-four people who lost their lives in the crash. His violin, it is said, remained intact.

Work

Many of the arrivals in June 1945, having been newly issued with clothing, were employed locally on the surrounding farms earning money, although around twenty per cent of them were classed as being unfit for work. Those classed as unfit included the older men who found the journey north taxing and the food grim, as well as those in hospital and those who simply were too dangerous to let out of the camp to work on the surrounding farms. One hundred and sixty-six of the prisoners were earning 2s. 6d. on average per week, while the rest were earning 5 shillings a week. This money could be used in the canteen to buy cigarettes, of which there were plenty, but there was little else they could purchase due to chronic shortages and rationing. The canteen's budget was set at £76 for the year, which meant every penny spent had to be done so wisely and had to be accounted for. To put that budget in context, the average weekly earnings for July 1945 for a British worker stood at £4 96s. 1d.

Work became a problem by November 1945. Fifteen officers and three non-commissioned officers, from Compound B, who were refusing to work, were put into a special hut surrounded by barbed wire. They had their own stove to cook their own food but because they were not willing to work their rations were specially calculated to take this into account. Full rations were given to all the men who worked, which was more food than they had been used to. Some had only been living on a few biscuits a day until their capture. The fifteen officers and their fellow objectors had all their privileges taken away too. They were no longer to have anything to do with the other prisoners for fear their actions would encourage others to refuse work. The ICRC inspector received a number of complaints from the interpreting sergeant regarding the attitude of the British personnel at the camp and he told Major Bieri, the ICRC inspector, they would only work if Lt.-Col. Murray, the camp's new commandant, heard their grievances. Many of the other prisoners were keen to work. From Compound A large numbers were working outside the camp in paid work in depots, in warehouses and in agricultural work. Some from Compound B were content to work inside the camp to pass the time, digging the garden or making repairs to huts. Lt.-Col. Murray informed the inspector at a meeting with him later that day that no one in the camp was forced to work, but because they had absented themselves for the moment, the men refusing to work warranted this segregation from the other prisoners. This despite the fact that of the men working from Compound A, fifteen per cent were making 3s. 4d. an hour with the rest making 1½d. an hour. From Compound B, thirty per cent of the men employed were making 1½d. an hour and the rest 3s. 4d. Walter Lindner and Hugo Fischer von Weikersthal, the heads of each compound, said that the men were able to do something useful for up to three hours a day.

Following on from the stand-off in Compound B in November 1945, the number of non-commissioned officers refusing to do work had risen to eighty-four by May 1946. This is not particularly surprising as more men had arrived in the camp and it was inevitable that some would protest about work. These men were transferred into Compound B, and apart from perhaps those suffering mental illness, these men would be doing camp administration duties. Other prisoners were billeted at the Transit Camp in Thurso, and at the RAF station, Burifa Hill at Dunnet Head, on administrative duties. According to Lt.-Col. Murray, 'Prisoners were also billeted on farms, about fifteen of whom elected to remain in Caithness and ninety to civilian status', he states in his account published in the local newspaper, the *John O'Groat Journal*. Civilian status meant the men no longer regarded themselves as part of the German military.

Work continued on the local farms for those prisoners who were allowed out. In May 1947 the Government introduced a scheme for the retention in approved cases only for German prisoners of war to remain on the farms where the farmer could provide accommodation and that it was seen in no way as detrimental to the local agricultural workers. In the joint announcement by the Ministry of Agriculture and the Department of Agriculture for Scotland, it stated that: 'The scheme will only apply to German prisoners of war who are or may be billeted on farms'. No German prisoner was to be given the option of becoming a civilian worker until he was given his form regarding his status for repatriation. However, the statement made it clear that any farmer who wanted to retain 'the services of a billeted prisoner of war as a civilian worker' would have to enter into the same kind of contract with the same terms and conditions as those expected by a British agricultural worker. It went on to say that the contract would only last until 31 December 1947, but that no immediate action needed to be taken. The farmers were going to be told by their local County War Agricultural Executive Committee and given the opportunity to apply to keep their billeted prisoners working on the farms as civilians from the date given to them for repatriation.

However, in Caithness a storm was brewing. A complaint was made at a County Council meeting when the local farmers were made aware that the prisoners who worked on their lands had been withdrawn. This had been done with absolutely no warning and the farmers felt that they were being deprived of the urgently needed labour force that had now been made unavailable to them. The Council decided to make a formal complaint to the Department of Agriculture over the matter. However, nothing was done. The Government had made its decision and the farmers would have to seek other men to work on the farms in the meantime.

By January 1948, when numbers had dwindled, most of the men remaining were in work with all from Compound A and eighty per cent of Compound B again busy on farms and in local businesses. Local farmers had chosen to ignore the Department of Agriculture and asked for the men to work for them. Consent was given by the camp.

One prisoner refused to work on Christmas Eve 1947 and by way of protest when he was put in detention went on hunger strike. This continued for the next week, however as the camp commandant, Lt.-Col. Murray saw it as his duty to have the man sent for treatment. He was taken to the infirmary on 1 January 1948 and force-fed. Although he was weak from the strike, the man made a full recovery.

The Food

The food at the camp was basic and because of wartime rations was sometimes disliked by the prisoners and guards alike. The menu consisted, for example, of oat flakes or porridge for break-fast with powdered milk, sugar and bread. Dinner was generally meat, potatoes and vegetables such as beans and a supper consisted of bread, margarine and perhaps sausages, served with tea. However, the German medical officer, Hegelmaier, was not at all impressed with the food. When asked about it he replied that it was not so good and he felt that it was having a detri-mental effect on the health of the men, although he said that generally their health was good. Rationing did not help the situation but there was also the other factor in that this was British food, not German, and the soldiers were simply not used to it.

Food rationing had been introduced in January 1940, although potatoes, oatmeal and seasonal vegetables were never rationed. The first foods rationed included bacon, sugar and butter, followed by tea, jam, eggs and sweets within two years. The Ministry of Food controlled the distribution of milk from the beginning of November 1941. National Dried Milk was introduced and mostly used in cooking. It did not taste anything like the fresh milk, but even in cooking it could still be tasted. Each person was allocated sixteen points worth of rationed goods in a month and they were allowed to choose how to use their points. However, basic rationing included a weekly allowance of, for example, 100 g (4 oz) of ham, 100 g of cheese, 100 g of margarine or butter and 225 g (8 oz) of sugar using the ration book coupons. Dried eggs were introduced in June 1942 and each packet, which had to do a family of four for four weeks, had the equivalent of 12 eggs in it. It was hard for everyone to adjust to the regime but it was out of necessity that it had been introduced and it continued for the new arrivals at Camp 165.

The food of the camp improved over the next year with the addition of some authentic German foodstuffs, such as Wiener Schnitzel. A typical menu now for Compound A consisted of cakes spread with butter-cream, soup, peas and carrots with salted potatoes, vanilla pudding, bread, fillet of fish served with tea or coffee. For Compound B, breakfast consisted of two cakes and tea, dinner was soup, Weiner Schnitzel, Leipziger Allerlei and a cold platter, again with tea. The overall view of the food was that it was very good, according to the senior medical officer Stabsarzt Meinhard Keizl. Having some German dishes, such as the Schnitzel, was seen as an olive branch and it was hoped this would be a sign of building the relationship between captors and captives. It could also have been seen as gesture of goodwill in that the British food still did not match the Germans' expectation of what good food was and this taste of German fare would have been greatly appreciated. This introduction of foreign food was the beginning of a massive change in Britain as a whole. The German, and other foreign nationals, had asked about food from their homelands and gradually some of the ingredients needed filtered through to the prisoner of war camps, where the camp cooks began experimenting. During the war, newspapers had advised the population on what to cook, but by 1946 attitudes had changed. People wanted new ideas and to get away from the war rationing system and soldiers returning had brought with them the delights of foreign cuisine. So as the Ministry of Food tried to keep the population adhering to the pretty drab food of the war years, prisoners began cooking their own traditional food from Germany, introducing it to the soldiers who guarded them. This major change in the attitude towards food was to continue for decades to come.

At Christmas 1946 the camp food was special for that day. During the previous few months, the men had cut down on margarine and other ingredients from their rations so that the food could be used at Christmas. In Compound A, the food consisted of coffee, butter-cream tart and apple tart for breakfast, fish soup, roast beef, gravy, potatoes and vegetables with a vanilla pudding with raisins for dinner, and a supper consisting of soup, cheese, sausages and sardines. A later supper was also offered of Streuselkuchen ['crumb cake' – a German speciality]. As a Christmas supplement, the men were also given twenty cigarettes, five bonus cigarettes, a small quantity of tobacco and cigarette papers, a mandarin orange, Gebäck, or fancy cakes, exercise books and a candle from the International Committee of the Red Cross.

In Compound B, most of the meals were the same with the exception of dinner. These men were offered soup, an appetiser of bread, roast beef, green vegetables and potatoes. For their

Christmas supplement, they had Stollen, Gebäck, an apple, a mandarin, coffee, twenty cigarettes and 20 g of tobacco courtesy of the International Committee of the Red Cross.

More German food was on the menu than ever before experienced. A real effort had been made to achieve this, not only by the saving up of their rations, but also by actually baking the food themselves in readiness for Christmas. It took much organisation but they managed this, much to their own satisfaction.

Health, Disease and Deaths

In June 1945 men in the camp infirmary were suffering from such ailments as diarrhoea, influenza, bronchitis and one man with a particularly heavy cold, and occupied seven of the beds. In March that year a soldier by the name of Kurt Thielecke had died from appendicitis due to the lack of medical equipment and medication. According to the medical officer, Oberarzt Wolf Hegelmaier, the medical supplies were now sufficient and there was a monthly inspection of the infirmary. The daily attendance on the sick parade was between fifteen and nineteen men. The dentist at the infirmary was Oberarzt Kuno Glockler and he carried out all dental work.

By November the new German medical officer, Stabsarzt Meinhard Keizl, noted that in the infirmary there were cases of gastro-intestinal catarrh, six cases of appendicitis, burns, boils, a leg tumour, eczema, angina and one case each of jaundice and a chronic inflammation of the eye, and one man who was diagnosed as being schizophrenic. One person was gravely ill with heart disease. Also noted was that one hundred of the prisoners were suffering from digestive problems but they seemed, in the most part, to be on the road to recovery. This was perhaps due to food poisoning from a reaction of some food with the dishes in which they were served. It is now known that a when certain foods were served in zinc bowls, a reaction took place which caused horrendous bouts of vomiting and diarrhoea. This reaction may have not been known then.

During January and February 1946 an influenza epidemic had gripped the camp with two hundred and seventy reported cases. One of these cases was fatal and Waffen-SS Obergruppenführer Jacob Lanzrath died on 17 of February. Only eighteen men out of over one thousand seven hundred were in the infirmary in June 1946: one suffering pneumonia, another suffering a swollen liver and another with a duodenum ulcer. The other illnesses included tonsillitis, influenza and one man had an abscess on his thigh. The number of beds in the infirmary had not increased to take onboard the new influx of prisoners and still stood at fifty.

In the winter of 1946–7 the usual round of winter ailments occurred. During Christmas 1946 nineteen out of the fifty beds were occupied but overall the general state of health in the camp was very good.

Over its three years as a prisoner of war camp, six men died whilst in captivity. These were Soldat Kurt Thielecke on 5 March 1945, who had appendicitis and subsequently died; Obergruppenführer Jacob Lanzrath on 17 February 1946 from complications related to influenza; Stabsgefeiter Ludwig Popp on 9 October 1946 who died of heart failure; Erich Kolleck on 15 January 1947 had internal burns, although what caused this is unknown; Oberführer Karl

Franz Balzer on 16 September 1947, aged fifty-seven from a heart attack; and Unteroffizier Fritz Tietgen died on 17 December 1947. He took his own life. He was forty-two years old.

One last prisoner has to be mentioned. On 8 of November 1946 a young prisoner lay wounded in the Dunbar Hospital in Thurso. Walter Helmut, who was just 20 years old, had suffered a gunshot wound to his leg whilst out at Strath, near to the prison camp. The shooting had occurred on the afternoon of Thursday 4 November. Whether the young soldier made a full recovery is unknown. There were rumours that a local farmer had shot him when he had seen the young German.

The Commandants

Lt.-Col. P. H. Drake-Brockham had been born in 1896 and was educated at Dover College. He was commissioned into the East Surrey Regiment in May 1915, serving as a member of the 1 Battalion in France and Belgium during World War I. During his time on the front, he was wounded three times. The East Surrey's suffered tremendous losses during that war. Out of the thirteen battalions that made up the East Surreys, over 6200 men, both officers and rank-and-file, were killed. From April 1918 until July 1919, Drake-Brockham, known simply as 'D-B', was employed by the Air Ministry and until 1936 he was with either 1st or 2nd Battalion, apart from a six year stint with the Royal West African Frontier Force. The RWAFF had been formed in 1900 in order to administer the regular colonial forces in West Africa. It consisted mainly of African troops made up from the Gold Coast Regiment, the Gambia Regiment, the Royal Sierra Leone Regiment and the Queen's Own Nigeria Regiment. In 1928 all these regiments became known as the Royal West African Frontier Force and it was with this Force that Drake-Brockham worked. From 1936 until the start of World War II, he was adjutant with the 5th (TA) Battalion, which changed its name to the 57th Anti-tank Regiment Royal Artillery, which went on to serve with the Desert Rats during the harsh fighting in North Africa. A year later, he was promoted to command the 50th Battalion, which over time, changed its name to the 11th Battalion then the 2nd Battalion, after the original Battalion had been forced to surrender to Japanese forces. But, in 1942, he was deemed too old for this duty and was so was posted out to the West Indies, where he raised and trained a battalion of fighting men. Sometime between then and May 1945, he returned to the United Kingdom and took over as Camp Commandant at prisoner of war Camp 165 in Watten.

Major Paris Hilary Drake-Brockham retired from the army on 21 December 1947, only a few months before the camp itself closed. He had spent his life dedicated to the army. He died on 19 September 1975 aged seventy-nine.

Lt.-Col. Rupert Luxmoore Tanner Murray, the second commandant of Camp 165, died unexpectedly in 1962, after an illustrious career with the Black Watch. In an obituary that appeared in the Black Watch's magazine *The Red Hackle*, his death was described as 'sudden'.

Murray had been educated at Wellington then went on to the Royal Military Academy Sandhurst at Camberley in Surrey and commissioned to the Black Watch just after the Armistice in 1918. He was posted to the 52nd Gordon Highlanders and went on to Köln, or Cologne, in Germany with them. Later he was sent to Curragh in Ireland with the Cameronians and spent two years there. The main reason the Cameronians were sent there was to crush the fledgling

Irish Republican Army, which had been established in 1919. The IRA sought the end of British rule in the north and for Ulster to be united with the rest of the county, using force as necessary. The hit-and-run-type guerrilla warfare, instigated by the IRA leader Michael Collins grew and hostilities quickly became worse and there was much bloodshed until finally a truce was reached in 1921. Over five hundred men on both sides had lost their lives in the two years of conflict.

During his tour of duty, the young 'Tishy' as he was affectionately known, took up cross-country running to add to his sporting interests. He was often seen running across Curragh Plain during his tour of duty and it was a sport he kept up. He was also a competent horse rider during hunts and enjoyed shooting. In May 1921, he was posted with the 2nd Battalion of the regiment to Silesia, where the rather thin Murray felt the cold penetrate his lean body and it is known he hated the Silesian winter. However, he took to theatrics to cheer himself up. Under the terms of the Treaty of Versailles, it was decided there should be a plebiscite in the disputed region of Upper Silesia; however, in 1921 the people wished to be part of Germany. This resulted in the Polish forces taking over a vast area of the region as the British troops were withdrawn. Germany, however, was not about to let the territory go without a fight. The Germans organised themselves to put up resistance against the Polish forces and it was at this time the British troops were sent back into the region, Murray among them. Eventually, the Silesian Question, as it was commonly known, was referred to the League of Nations, where a small committee of delegates from only four countries decided that Poland should receive one third of the territory but half the population and most of the industry. This would later become a factor in the outbreak of World War II.

In 1925 'Tishy' and the 2nd Battalion had returned to Scotland, to Fort George near Inverness, where he and his battalion sports team won the Scottish Command Cup. His cross-country running was still a favourite sport. He was able to pursue his other passion for shooting in his spare time and apparently was an excellent shot.

During the 1930s, Murray enhanced the Regimental Club in Edinburgh, which had fallen foul of neglect. According to *The Red Hackle*, Murray 'acquired new quarters in a respectable neighbourhood, procured new trustees and responsible members of a Committee, set the Club on a sound financial footing and gave it an impetus that it never lost'. He raised funds for the Club and according to the report, 'these years in Edinburgh were probably the happiest period of his adult life'. His fund raising had one very memorable occasion. He had organised a dance at Dundas Castle near Dalmeny with the full blessing of the hosts, the Stewart-Clarks, but the weather was to play havoc with the guests' travelling arrangements. It was the foggiest night there had been in the Forth Valley for a long time and the only guests at the castle were Murray and his mother, for the rest could not see their way clear to reach the venue. Eventually some guests did arrive but only after great difficulty. Many did not, but apparently the fundraiser was able to add a substantial amount of money for the cause anyway, thanks to the Stewart-Clarks.

In 1937 the 2nd Battalion was sent to Palestine and Murray was promoted to major on 1 October 1938. Palestine, it had been proposed, had to be partitioned and that separate states, one for Arabs and one for Jews, be established. There had been disturbances in the area, as a mandate on the British colony was long awaited about a final outcome of the situation. An Arab rebellion had begun in 1936 and Murray's regiment was sent out there to do a tour of duty as a peacekeeping force. While on its way out there, the 2nd Battalion encountered transportation problems, as the convoys did little more than ten miles an hour and broke down constantly. Murray was appointed Military Transport Officer and it was not too long before the convoys were moving steadily along at thirty miles an hour with few breakdowns. Inspecting officers sent back glowing reports on the battalion military transport and just before war broke out the Brigade Commander described it as being 'excellent' and it was due to Murray.

During World War II, Murray was commander of a Pioneer Company when he was captured on the island of Crete and interned in a prisoner of war camp until his release in 1945. As a prisoner of war, he became very ill with dysentery and it did not help that the rations were so poor that his slender body merely became weaker. However, he survived. His experiences subsequently stood him in good stead for his new role in Caithness, as he understood the needs of prisoners from firsthand experience and the risk of diseases and their effects on the men. During his time in captivity, he had become a temporary lieutenant-colonel as he had automatically succeeded his group commander. When the men were liberated, they returned to Scotland and were brought up to date at Dunbar before being given new posts. Murray was to head prisoner of war camps, his first posting to a camp in Edinburgh then to Watten.

Murray was held in high regard at Watten. He was seen as fair and just and is still remembered fondly by former prisoners and guards alike.

Chapter 3

A Prisoner's Story

In the summer of 2005 Herr Ludwig Schoon was holidaying with a local family in Caithness. Since his time at *Lager* 165, he had struck up a relationship with the Storm family that has lasted more than sixty years. When he comes to Scotland, he stays with the family for an average of four weeks. His first return was in 1997. What follows is his story.

Ludwig Schoon was born in Leer in north-western Germany in August 1926. When he was just seventeen years old he was conscripted into the German army and was captured in France when he was part of the 12 Panzer Grenadier Division. This Division had been set up in 1943 and on 1 of May that year, eight thousand Hitlerjugend volunteers began their six week pre-basic training and some were sent to special training camps. These boys had a strong belief in the Third Reich and its leader and were willing to fight until the death so that Germany would win the war. By September 1943 the Hitlerjugend had over sixteen thousand fully-trained fighting boys. Although these seventeen- and eighteen-year-olds were prepared, fully fit and ready for action, veterans from the Eastern Front were brought in, many of whom came from the 1st SS Panzer Division, known as the Leibstandarte Adolf Hitler. These soldiers taught the young recruits how to fight, using real-life scenarios and live weapons training.

Herr Schoon had served most of his time in the army in Belgium at the military training camp at Beverloo before being sent to northern France just before the Allied landings of 6 June 1944. The 12th SS Panzers came under heavy and prolonged attack from the British and Canadian forces which had landed at the beaches codenamed Juno and Sword earlier in the day and had reached Caen. After the liberation of Caen, the 12th SS Panzers became encircled at the area known as the Falaise Pocket, where many German combat divisions were trapped. The Panzers finally escaped from encirclement a month after the Allied invasion, only for many German soldiers to be killed or captured. Upon his capture, Herr Schoon remembers the differing attitudes of the soldiers. He found the Polish troops to be harsh and unfriendly, but the 'British troops were fairest in the war'. He stayed in France for another three weeks, living without shelter of any kind and eating rations of two biscuits and a pot of tea for two twice a day. 'The heavens were our tent', as he puts it. After that he was shipped across to England to Camp 136, at Welton, a small village five miles from Hull, where the men were deloused. Lice were a constant problem during the war. Easily transmitted from soldier to soldier, infestation was impossible to control due to the lack of proper amenities: however, methods were available to control lice such as fumigation chambers, but not in the field. The best the men could do was comb their hair and pull the lice off with their fingers. This method did not work, nor did washing their hair with the little soap they had available as the lice clung on. Some of the men found that oil or grease helped to keep them at bay but it was only a matter of time before re-infestation. Shelter at Welton came in the form of tents, for the camp had no place to facilitate the new arrivals since it was in the grounds to the east of the manor house. Temporary huts were built there but not enough of them for the new internees.

From there, before the winter of 1944–45 set in, Herr Schoon was sent to Le Marchant Camp at Devizes known as Camp 23. Camp 23 was where he was to find notoriety with the greatest escape plan ever hatched from a prisoner of war camp on the British mainland.

The Devizes breakout plan involved the recently arrived German prisoners caught in France. They were some of the most hard-line Nazis who were optimistic at a time when the regular soldier was fully aware that the war was coming to an end. Certain in their belief that Germany could still win the war, these men would never give up even though they had been captured and were now prisoners of war in an enemy country. In the German sergeant-major's office the escape was meticulously planned. They had discovered a weak area in the camp's fencing, and a close watch was kept on the truck movements. They were checking the locks in the compound, keeping a careful note of what came in at what times and who was involved in checking and unloading the trucks. Christmas week was chosen for the escape attempt. It was hoped that because the patrols in the camp would be lighter as some guards would be on Christmas leave, and those on duty perhaps distracted by thoughts of home and families, and their morale would be low. Escape by the prisoners would be relatively simple if the guards had only half their thoughts on their duties. The plan was as follows. A selection of truck drivers would commandeer vehicles and break into the arms store. Food was to be taken from the food stores and loaded onto some of the other trucks. Once the armed prisoners were ready to move, the breakout would happen. From the camp, the plan was to drive north to pick up more escaped prisoners of war and with their numbers increased they would head east and radio to Germany to be picked up. Unfortunately for the men, the plot was uncovered by a vigilant German-speaking American based at the camp. He had overheard soldiers talking about it in hushed voices and had been keen to hear more. Slowly he had made his way to a vantage point and listened to their discussion of the truck situation and the amassing of the forces from the other camps. He reported what he had heard. A search was ordered and weaponry was found hidden in beds and under the ground. The thirty or so leaders were interrogated then transferred to the London District Cage (LDC) for further investigation. The LDC in Kensington became notorious as a place of alleged torture where German combatants were said to have been deprived of sleep which with other methods was used to extract information about what the British intelligence services believed these men knew. Much of what happened at the Cage has been disputed over the years by historians, and no clear picture exists that torture did in fact take place, but bullying certainly did occur. It was at the Cage that the fate of one young man was about to be meted out.

Two men fell under suspicion as being traitors to the plan. One suffered at the hands of his co-accused there and then, with the British allowing him to be beaten quite savagely before it was stopped and he was not killed. The other was a man whose name is synonymous with British camps. He was Wolfgang Rosterg, a liberal German, who was in fact innocent of the crime of which he was accused. Unfortunately, he with other, more ardent Nazi colleagues, was sent to Camp 21 at Cultybraggan near Comrie in Perthshire, Scotland, which was very like Watten camp as it was far from centres of population in wild countryside in the middle of nowhere. This camp too held the very Nazis that were hated so much by Britain and her Allies. They held their beliefs of nationalist socialism with unconditional loyalty to Hitler and his regime. It was said that any man who appeared at the camp and did not show this kind of abiding loyalty to the Fatherland was a marked man from the moment his beliefs were uncovered. Comrie was, at the end of 1944, the highest security prisoner of war camp in Britain. It was here Rosterg stirred up things when he criticised the way the Germans had fought at the Ardennes. Hitler's chief in the west, Field Marshall Karl von Rundstedt, as well as the Commander-in-Chief of Army Group B, Walter Model, had voiced their concerns that the plan was unrealistic, and although the Battle of the Bulge started well for the German offensive, the Allies, especially the Americans, succeeded in forcing the retreat. Rosterg had merely voiced his opposition to the foolhardiness of the plan and agreed with the reservations of von Rundstedt. However, his reputation as an anti-Nazi was already well known in England and some of the men sent with him to Scotland had already probably set about engineering his fate. On his arrival at Comrie, a group of prisoners was suspicious of him too, as he made no secret of his distaste for other Nazi policies and the Nazi leadership. His lack of enthusiasm was also clear as he was one of only a very few men who did not salute Hitler but derided him. He was a marked man from the start. On the night of 23 December, he paid for his views with his life.

A so-called committee of prisoners dragged him from his bed and questioned him all night, beating him at times. They asked him about spying for the British, and taunted him with any homemade weapon they could find. Just before morning, a rope was produced and he was dragged to the washroom where he was strung up and left to die. Exhausted by the torture, he had put up no fight. The torturers knew they would never get away with the crime but they were so completely consumed by the Nazi propaganda with which they had been indoctrinated over the years, they saw it as their duty to Adolf Hitler to remove anyone who did not support him and his policies. Eight men were later sent to the LDC where five of them, Erich Konig, Josep Mertens, Kurt Zuelsdorf, Joachim Golitz and Heinz Brueling, were found guilty of the murder and were hanged in Pentonville prison in London for their crime on 8 October 1945. Only Mertens showed any regret for the crime. It was at Devizes where these events began to unfold and it was to that camp that Ludwig Schoon had arrived – and it was freezing.

Devizes itself lies deep in the Wiltshire countryside. The camp was positioned on a road running out of the town towards the Marlborough Downs and was once a prison but in 1944 it was home to thousands of German prisoners of war and Herr Schoon was one of them.

He remembers the day he arrived at the camp and describes the freezing conditions: 'The temperature was about ten degrees below in wintertime. Every day we got a pail of coal. That meant a little bit of warmth for three hours around a stove.' But the harsh winter weather continued and the men wrapped up as much as they could to keep warm. Even physical exercise did not put much heat into them, nor did the food they were given. Eventually spring came and conditions improved.

Herr Schoon arrived at Camp 165 in Watten in the autumn of 1945 and was there for ten months. He had travelled up by train, which took several days and finally arrived in the middle of the night. His initial allocation was to Compound B. In common with all the men, he was issued with clothing, a sleeping bag, two blankets and a special number. Every prisoner of war was allocated this number and told to remember it. Ludwig's number was A774391. 'My whole life, I never forgot this number', Herr Schoon declares. 'This number was more important than our name.'

'We had the same clothes like the British Army, but the suit we got was dark brown. In the back of the jacket was cut a hole, which was covered with a lightly-coloured patch. The same happened with the trousers. In the camp we were also allowed to wear German uniforms.' The reason for the patches was so that the prisoners could be easily identified as such, although it has been suggested the patches were a symbolic gesture of dislike by the British authorities who compared it to the Star of David worn by the Jews in continental Europe. Yet many of these young recruits were well liked and were well behaved so it is unlikely this was the case.

Herr Schoon remembers the winter

> The winter in Watten was not very cold. That was very good for us. The barracks and Nissen huts in every camp were in very poor condition and it meant the possibility of heat. The Nissen hut was mostly cold but we were used to this temperature. It was the same in every camp until 1948 [when he was repatriated] … In the wintertime, we got a little bit of coal to warm us.

If the winter in Watten had been like that of 1955, when Caithness was hit by one of the biggest snowfalls in living memory, all of the prisoners would have fared much worse.

He goes on to describe the interior of his accommodation.

> The front side had a door and two windows. Inside, in the middle, was a corridor and on both sides of the corridor were bunk beds. I can't remember how many of them. I think on one side five and the other side four with a place for the small stove. I think there were about eighteen men living in the hut. There was a stove, but no table, wardrobe or cupboard. We could not put up pictures, although most prisoners of war had no photos as they had either lost them or they had been taken away. The wall was made from metal and had the form of waves. At the back of the hut there was also a door and a window. Behind the door was a small toilet that was to be used during the night. The guards got the order to shoot on us during the night but the guards never did follow this order.

Herr Schoon touches here on probably one of the less pleasant sides of the British army. Due to the horrors seen by the British in Germany and the stories they brought back with them, it was not at all unusual for them to strip the German soldiers of personal possessions as a kind of punishment. Word reached home about the concentration camps, about the brutality carried out by some German guards on Allied prisoners, and about such incidents as the shooting of eighty Allied prisoners of war in a barn in Wormhoudt, northern France. The British had to be seen to be treating the prisoners fairly but this stripping of photographs, medals and letters was fairly common practice.

He stresses that the 'camp was ok. We had a wonderful commander. We spent the days walking round, and walking round. There were many football players. There were four football clubs and every four weeks they had a football festival. It was absolutely no problem'. The young men had built up a relationship with the camp guards and Lt.-Col. Murray and they proved themselves, on the whole, to be no trouble therefore they were allowed to participate in the football matches as mentioned. Local people used to go along and watch as these young foreigners played. Later, the prisoners were allowed to play against a team from Thurso known as the Swifts.

One major complaint the prisoners had was about the food in the camp. They were not used to British food and it was not the best of fare they were receiving. However that was no different from the rest of the population, who were also unhappy about the food and the continuing rationing. Herr Schoon remembers the food well:

> The food in Camp B was very bad and after some months there was an irritable atmosphere in the camp. Therefore the German camp leader, Hauptfeldswebel Hugo Fischer von Weikersthal, and a delegation, asked to see the commandant to discuss the situation. Afterwards, on the order of the commander, everyone in Camp B had to be weighed. The result was that we were all 10–20% underweight. I can't remember whose fault it had been but, afterwards, the food became much better.

However, Herr Schoon never forgot the camp porridge which was served every morning. Never again once he left Watten did he have it.

It was clear that the men had been receiving the wrong amount of food for a fairly sustained time. Whether it was a miscalculation or not, it meant they were malnourished and urgent action was requested by Murray to make sure the rations were upped to their correct quantity for the men of Compound B. Fairly quickly, the men gained weight. Added to that was the fact that the food began to improve. This mistake in rations was never again to happen in Camp 165.

However, the weight gain was halted for a few days as the men recovered from a severe case of food poisoning. Although food poisoning did occur occasionally in camps, there were only ever a few cases, but on this occasion, the incidence was of mammoth proportions:

> One Sunday, after dinner, we got a dessert, which did not happen very often. It was a simple pudding but had been put into metal bowls. In these zinc bowls, oxidation must have taken place so the pudding was poisoned. The following night, everyone got horribly ill with diarrhoea. The next morning everybody had to visit the doctor in Camp A, and to all of us he said the same thing: 'Black tea and toasted bread'. There was to be no medication.

Ludwig Schoon, a prisoner of Camp 165, retains close ties with Caithness to this day.

For several days, the men suffered. Some could not keep down even the tea and toast to begin with, but as time wore on they managed. At any given time, the latrines were busy for the next twenty-four hours. Never again was the camp to suffer from the same fate.

As for passing the time, Herr Schoon joined in with the camp's educational classes.

> In the first year I learnt English. I learned nearly perfect English. Learn, learn, learn. Dreaming in the night, I will learn English. It is very interesting to learn English when you are young. Then you forget it, but I didn't forget. I had to learn English to understand what was being said. The camp teacher was very good.

As testimony to that teacher, he reiterated that 'I learned nearly perfect English'. This was the first time in his life he had ever studied the language.

Many of the prisoners felt the same way as Herr Schoon. When they had arrived, many spoke either no English or very little, therefore they could not fully understand what was being said. By leaning the language, they slowly began to make sense of the instructions given to them or could strike up conversations with the guards.

Another way of passing the time was writing back home to Germany. Although some officers had difficulties and were not allowed to write home, Herr Schoon was no threat whatsoever to national security and not wanted for any war crimes, and was permitted this privilege.

> We were allowed to send letters home. We got one letter every month. It was specially printed for prisoners of war, and we also got a postcard. It was not allowed that we write about the camp and also not allowed to say which district of Britain the camp was. The postal service took a long time before these arrived home in Germany.

But arrive they did and they let family members know that their loved ones, although incarcerated, were safe. Letters in the main spoke of pastimes, such as football matches and studying, but as Herr Schoon rightly states, no information about the camp or its location was allowed at that time, although later, this was not the case, as letters were marked specifically to POW Compound 165, Watten, Caithness, Northschottland, England, as one parcel was addressed in 1947. Scores of people in continental Europe, especially in Germany, addressed many of the letters as 'Schottland, England', as it was the case that England was the term used for the whole of the United Kingdom. The main point was that the letters got through, eventually, and it gave the prisoners hope, although some received news from home about the conditions there and were disheartened.

Just before Herr Schoon was sent away from Camp 165 he had begun work on a local farm, at Lythmore. Betty Storm, niece of John Dunnett who owned the farm, keeps in touch with Ludwig, something that Ludwig himself started when he left Caithness. She was about sixteen years old when she met Ludwig Schoon and the other prisoners who worked on the farm. They would come out to the farm every morning and on one occasion they removed the engine from John Dunnett's car, fixed the problem and replaced it in good working order. Herr Schoon returned to Caithness in 1997 for the first time in over 50 years.

> I never forget this time in Scotland. I never forget my time here. My wife died in 1996 and I said to my sons that I want to go back to Scotland. The

boys said ok. I came in August 1997 and stayed with Betty. She is fantastic.

On one of his visits, he explains about a curious incident that happened when he was on his way to see Betty. At an airport, the plane broke down.

> I reached Gatwick airport, but there was a breakdown and we had to return to the airport. I sat at a table and was having some food. A man came over to the table and we started to talk. I told him I was worried I would miss my train connection to Caithness and was a former prisoner of war. He told me he had been one of the guards at the camp in 1946 and was also heading home to Caithness. Since then, we have a good friendship.

Herr Schoon returns to Caithness to stay with Betty for holidays and is known affectionately by the family as Lewis. He speaks of his time on the farm with a great deal of fondness and explains how he came to go there.

> Colonel Murray was very good. He was very fair. Murray had been a prisoner of war in Germany and was the commander of this camp – Camp 165. He was a wonderful commander. There were two camps to begin with. The first camp was Number 1 camp. They could go working. Number 2 camp couldn't go. They had been in the Hitler Youth. The Hitler Youth were not nice people. They weren't democratic. We were in 'A', 'B', 'C' and 'C+'. 'A' held the super democrats. [By this Herr Schoon means that they were willing to change the government for one that was not a dictatorship, but one that actually listened to the people and was voted in democratically.] In 'C', the British army held members of the Nazi Party and Hitler Youth. There were lots of submariners there. I stayed ten months in the camp and gave no trouble. I went to Camp 1 and tried to go to work on farms. I didn't know this work. I had a great time. After three months on the farm, I was sent to England and got home in 1948. Betty too was a good teacher of English.

Life on the farm gave Herr Schoon a sense of worth. He was young and willing to undertake any task asked of him. He worked hard and was content to learn about this new skill of farming. It also helped that the family he worked with were so kind and helpful to him. This was something for which he was grateful.

As for the people of Caithness as a whole, Herr Schoon could not understand why they were so compassionate towards their enemy. He had spent time in England where the attitude was very different from that of Caithness, where people, although they did not forget what had happened during the war, were willing to accommodate the young men by allowing them into their homes and being part of their lives.

> I couldn't understand how they were so kind. England was a problem. The people were not so good. I had no chance, no money. Here, there was no trouble with the civilian people. They bore no grudge and gave us a lot of hope. I remember a little boy on a German prisoner's lap. The prisoner said, 'One spoon for you, one for me', and so it went on. The people were just so friendly.

This is testament to the kindness of strangers to each other and the humanity and compassion that brought them together. Here were foreign nationals, a long way from their homeland, making an ever deeper and lasting impression on the people of Caithness by simply being themselves. The story of the little boy is one that sums up the attitudes of both sides, where trust and friendship have come together in the innocence of the child, who obviously was delighted by the attention he was being shown. Such stories are not uncommon in the area.

However, life had its difficulties and depressing times for all of the men as they wanted to be repatriated. The war was over and they had hoped to be returned to Germany quickly. This was not to happen, until the British government was sure the men would return to Germany with a new way of thinking. Herr Schoon explains the feelings of the soldiers

> We were very depressed, not that the war was finished, but about our future. We were convinced we would have to stay there [in captivity] a long, long time; and three and a half years was a long, long time.

He was not alone in this outlook. Many of the soldiers longed to go home to their families and it was the not knowing when this was going to happen that drove some of them to despair. Some had spent most of the war as prisoners and felt they had paid enough by being held captive. They considered themselves as free men now the hostilities had ended yet here they were still held in a barbed wire cage. When first captured, these men had been told they would spend three months in the United Kingdom and now felt deceived by the authorities. The younger and more fanatical ones reacted badly to this. They saw themselves as heroes and martyrs and the general feeling amongst them was one of injustice at being held for so long. They had lost families and friends and wanted to return home as soon as possible since the war was over.

During his incarceration after Watten, Herr Schoon remembers how a change in the law occurred which meant that the no fraternisation rule with the people in Great Britain was revoked. It was the case of a girl becoming pregnant to one of the prisoners of war that changed attitudes.

> The British girl became pregnant by a German prisoner. He was arrested and put into prison. But the British girl didn't accept that. She wrote a letter to Queen Elizabeth, the Queen Mother, and also informed the press. After some weeks, this law was cancelled and so she was allowed to marry her German friend.

This type of incident was not unique. From many of the camps, local girls and the prisoners fraternised covertly and some, as in the case mentioned above, had happy married lives together. During the war and immediately afterwards, it was forbidden for people to interact with the prisoners without prior permission, and it was most certainly out of bounds to have an intimate relationship with them. Yet it was impossible to enforce the non-fraternisation. With the sense of danger ever present, the young women, not only of Caithness, but also all over the British Isles, had secret rendezvous with the dashing young German soldiers. To begin with, the girls would speak to the soldiers as they passed the camp after a wolf whistle or a salutation, which would then progress into stopping and chatting briefly. Eventually, in the dark of night, they would meet. Partly out of danger, partly sympathy and possibly empathy, this continued throughout the life of Camp 165. The soldiers would make small gifts for the girls and the girls would bring some extra food for the soldiers. If either had been caught, they would have been severely reprimanded for their actions.

Ludwig Schoon was finally repatriated via a camp in England and found that when he returned home, Germany had changed out of all recognition, with many of the houses in his area having been taken over by Polish families. It was a devastating blow.

> A lot of Polish workers during the war had come to work on farms, in factories and stayed. Polish troops came to our districts. The Polish soldiers told the people to leave their houses for the Polish people.

This happened during his enforced stay in Watten as refugees flooded Europe from the east.

> In 1948 the Polish people left the north-west part of Germany for Canada. The Polish and Canadians were not so good. I remember the commander of the Poles was Canadian.

The Polish people, it must be remembered, hated the Germans for their invasion in 1939, but also there was a long history of distrust and abhorrence between the two nations. Germany had tried several times to make Poland part of the German Empire and attempted to destroy her people so the Germanic peoples could take over the land, to create a Greater Germany.

Herr Schoon recalls the time when Hitler came to power:

> Before the war, we were told there would be no war again. But then there was. We were all disappointed. I spent several years in France and was captured by the British. The Polish troops were difficult, but the British troops were the fairest in the war. The Hitler Youth were told that they would never go back to Germany. The Commander told us that they would never come back. As time went on, the war was, year by year, forgotten. We learned governments make war, not people.

Herr Schoon had grown up under the influence of Nazism and in the shadow of the Third Reich and Hitler Youth. Hitler came to power when Herr Schoon was just six years old and he was held in Scotland from the age of eighteen. He was an SS soldier of ordinary rank and had the typical blond hair and blue eyes of the Aryan race which Hitler had thought to be so desirable. Many locals have commented on the appearance of these soldiers. A mass of blond heads was highly unusual in Caithness and caused much speculation. As time went on, many were integrated into Caithness society and still, over sixty years later, have strong links with the locals. It bears out the fact that most of the soldiers who were allowed to leave the camp to work locally were accepted wholeheartedly after an initial reticence.

Even after he had been repatriated, there were severe problems when he wanted to return to Scotland for a visit. German people, whether they wanted to visit Scotland or get married here, had to fight for that right. One couple spent over two years writing letters almost weekly to the local provost, and letters to the Foreign Office, endeavouring to gain permission to be married. 'Later, I couldn't get permission to come over. I never got permission to go to Holland. The civilian planes of Lufthansa and BA didn't fly.' As a result he had a long wait. His patience was rewarded and he finally returned fifty years after his first stay in the county.

Finally Herr Schoen crystallises the attitude of the British government of the day: 'No one was allowed to write about the camp. Not much was said about it.'

The above has been said by many people, and it is confirmed by a former prisoner of war. Secrecy has surrounded Camp 165 Watten for nearly sixty years. Why this should be the case is unclear in today's world. However in the world of the 1940s, it was easily understood when so many of the Third Reich's top commanders were incarcerated in British prisoner of war camps.

Watten has left its mark on Herr Schoon, and when he was told he was leaving Camp 165 in 1946, he says he was sad to go because he enjoyed working on the farms and playing football. Today, this former prisoner has a very special place in his heart for his 'old enemies'.

Chapter 4

Escapes

Throughout the camp system in the United Kingdom, there were numerous escape attempts. The biggest attempt was made by Italian prisoners held at Camp 112, Bun Camp, at Doonfoot in Ayrshire in December 1944. In total ninety-seven of the prisoners escaped through a tunnel they had dug out for months, but all of them were recaptured quickly. Another attempt was made by sixty-seven German prisoners of war at Camp 198 in Bridgend, Wales, known as Island Farm on 10 March 1945. Again, they were all recaptured quickly. However, the most daring came from Le Marchant, as already mentioned in the previous chapter, and Lodge Moor camps, where the hardcore Nazi prisoners planned a breakout, and intended to march on London. These were thwarted.

During the lifetime of the camp at Watten there were several escape attempts. The first of these occurred only a few months after its designation as prisoner of war Camp 165. However, Lt.-Col. Murray not only instructed his men to find the prisoners, but also took part in looking for them himself, driving around in his own private car. Indeed he recaptured some, throwing them into the car and returning to the camp.

The roads around the camp were generally single track, with the exception of the main route between Wick and Thurso, the A882. The closest road to the camp is what is now numbered the B870 between the village and Mybster, a tiny hamlet now on the main A9 route, meandering its way over the countryside, through the fields and past smallholdings and crofts. This route rises to a small plateau over which the loch at Watten is clearly visible. To the south the mountains of Sutherland rise and to the east lies the Moray coastline, dotted with former fishing communities.

On a daily basis, more and more prisoners arrived at Watten, travelling north past these places, with the original five hundred and one having been shipped off to camps elsewhere and new internees arriving at the end of July and August. The new inmates took time to adjust to their new surroundings. With the war being over in Europe, these men must have thought that they would soon be heading back to Germany and therefore questioned their imprisonment as time went on. It would have been difficult, especially for the younger ones who had been conscripted into the forces, to understand the delay. Unperturbed, some of them hatched their plans and hoped escaping from the camp would mean a journey home.

On 27 of August 1945 the first escape attempt took place. The unnamed young man broke out of the camp in the early hours of the morning, tramping his way across fields and tracks until he reached the main road south. It must be noted that in August the skies only get inky black dark for a few hours between roughly eleven o'clock at night and perhaps three o'clock in the morning, so when he left on his expedition in the morning, he would have been able to see where he was going. He must have felt so isolated in the Caithness countryside because for miles and miles the land stretches out with few places to shelter and no distinctive landmarks. A few derelict crofts may have provided some form of shelter but many of these were inland of the road and it would have been easier for the prisoner to stick close to the highway. The route he must have taken would have been fairly direct, passing Strath and the Grey Cairns of Camster, until he reached a fishing village fourteen miles from the camp. The Neolithic cairns had been excavated in the nineteenth century and may have provided the young soldier with shelter, as the central chamber in the round cairn was intact. It is possible he spent an hour or so in there, eating some of the little rations he had saved from mealtime and resting before daybreak before continuing his trek south, and on to freedom. On the last part of his fateful journey he must have been relieved to see the coast. However, when he reached the village of Latheron, he was spotted sitting at the roadside by Special Constable James Fraser, who was the Governor of the County Home for the Poor in the village. The young soldier was still wearing his German uniform so was easily identifiable. Mr Fraser notified the local policeman, Constable Kennedy, and the soldier was soon arrested. Although he was over six feet tall, and likely to have been incredibly fit, he was exhausted and hungry so he offered the constable no resistance and was returned to the camp after just ten hours of freedom.

Three prisoners, all of who were formerly members of the German navy, contrived the next escape attempt. The men had gathered and formulated a plan and managed to execute it on the night of 13 May 1946. Like the attempt made in August 1945, the skies were fairly light and the men had judged when the best time would be to leave the camp. In the early hours, the submariners gathered together, using hand signals to each other as their only form of communication. They had worked out that guards would be half asleep at around three in the morning as that was the lowest ebb for any human being. Silently, they took it in turn and gathered together a few belongings and food with one of them always on guard, watching the movements of the patrolling guards. As they left the Nissen hut, the sun was just beginning to rise, giving them enough light to see where they were going. They pulled at the barbed wire and eased themselves through out onto the field beyond. Using the cover of some bushes, they waited a few minutes but heard no commotion and knew they had made it safely out of the compound. Running across the fields, they made their bid for freedom.

The guards raised the alarm as soon as they discovered the men were missing at roll call. Sentries from the camp scoured the Caithness countryside for them, in the hope that due to the nature of the rural idyll their concealment would be incredibly difficult. Added to that,

The wilderness of Dorrery provided little shelter for escaped prisoners.

the weather had turned and the conditions were horrendous. The guards knew there were few places where the men could shelter and supposed they would be soaked through, with their morale severely dented. If they were sheltering somewhere, it would be in a barn or a derelict croft, for the guards knew the local people would report anyone found hiding in their homes. Described as wearing their grey uniforms and green overcoats, and only one of them being able to speak little English, the guards were sure that the prisoners would soon be returned to camp. Unbeknown to the marines, their escapade was nearly over.

Having been on the run for seventy-two hours, they were recaptured at Lybster, a small fishing village some twenty or so miles from the camp on the eastern Caithness coast. Lybster had been a thriving herring port, in fact the third largest in Scotland, founded by Lt General Patrick Sinclair in the 1700s, but by the 1940s the fishing industry had begun to decline and with so many of the villagers off fighting in Europe, the boats remained tied up.

Two young men who were returning from a dance in the village at one o'clock in the morning had spotted the submariners huddled together trying to shelter. The men had informed the local police that they had seen the Germans and a search began immediately. However, by the time the search got underway, the fugitives had disappeared.

The submariners had also seen the young men and knew they would be reported. They quickly gathered their belongings together and ran. The obvious place to go was the harbour, for they had seen the fishing boats and knew they could hide in one. But they also knew it would be the first place the search parties would look. They had no choice but to go overland and hope they found some form of hiding place.

The hunt continued throughout the night, but to no avail. Polish troops, who were stationed locally at Skitten and Castletown, were enlisted to help the following day – 16 May. They combed the area towards the south as it was assumed it would be the direction the men would have taken. The search proved tricky when they reached the marshy lands at Swiney. Nevertheless one of their patrols found the men, hiding in an uninhabited house at the top of Swiney Hill, which lies roughly a mile south of Lybster. When found, the three men were exhausted and offered no resistance to the troops. They gestured to the troops that they were unarmed and that there would be no confrontation. They rose to their feet and were thoroughly checked before being led from the house. They were then manhandled and escorted back to Watten in the back of a truck by British soldiers. The Polish troops were friendly towards the men, but on their return, the camp guards were somewhat infuriated by their escape and treated them rather less pleasantly. They were stripped of their wet clothes, given some warm food then confined to barracks as punishment. It is amazing none suffered from the effects of exposure or hypothermia given the climatic conditions.

A minor escape occurred four months later when two former SS men made it as far as Dorrery near Scotscalder in the heart of the Caithness countryside. They had followed the line of the railway, trudging over Bloody Moss, crossing at the Scotscalder railway junction and ending up on the moorland at Dorrery. At Dorrery there is no village or hamlet, only a scattering of farms, Dorrery Lodge and a few surrounding lochs, which would have supplied the men with drink, but there was nowhere to shelter in the barren landscape. For miles around there is nothing but undulating land with little relief from the moorland winds. Hiding at the local farms was out of the question for the farmers would have just called in the police. The SS soldiers had chosen the wrong direction to go in. If they had followed the railway line south at Scotscalder instead of branching off, they may have been able to jump on a train as it slowly gained its speed coming out of the station, but this was not to be. They were captured on Thursday 16 September 1946 and returned to the camp. It was rumoured in the county some time after the news broke locally that the two SS men had laid out a swastika on the ground as a signal for the German forces to come to their aid and rescue them. However this was untrue. No German flag had been smuggled into the camp and even if the soldiers had tried to get one through on their arrival, it would have been confiscated.

The next night, following in the footsteps of the SS, another three men escaped. They were recaptured a day later at Thrumster, a hamlet twelve miles from the camp, which lies four miles to the south of the county town of Wick. At that time, the light railway line ran between Wick and Lybster. Perhaps these men thought they could catch a train to take them further south. To reach Thrumster, the easiest route for the soldiers would have been along the main road between Watten and Wick, cutting off at the tiny hamlet of Haster, yet if they had done that, they would surely have been spotted, therefore they must have trudged over fields to reach as far as Thrumster.

The first recorded escape in 1947 took place in mid-May when two prisoners from Watten went on the run for forty-eight hours. An opportunistic escape, this was not pre-planned. The men had discussed escape before but had not thought about it seriously until the occasion arose. When it did, they took their chances and had headed off. They had followed the railway track south and had gone onto the heath land when they passed villages so they would not be caught. Lying in amongst the heathers gave them just enough cover not to be seen by villagers getting on with their daily business. The northern line from Wick to Inverness weaves its way inland from Watten, covering Scotscalder, Altnabreac to Forsinard then turns south taking in Kinbrace, Kildonan and Helmsdale in Sutherland, before following the coast down as far as Golspie and returning inland again. However, the two prisoners got as far as Kildonan, a tiny rural community west of Helmsdale. They had been seen tramping over the moorland by the wife of the local railway porter, who reported it. However, before the police arrived on the scene, the men were challenged by three local men and, without putting up any resistance, were captured. They were taken back to Camp 165.

This is a recurring theme with Camp 165. Whenever the men who had escaped were caught, not once did they put up any resistance when challenged face to face. Occasionally it may have been because they were outnumbered or the police had caught them and they did not want to make things any worse than they already were. A prisoner of war camp was one thing, but prison was something else. Most of the time, however, it seems to be the case it was simply because they were hungry and exhausted.

The most notable escape took place on Monday 18 August 1947. Soldat A. Nohr, aged 28, and Soldat T. Verborg, a year older than his companion, both of whom were from the German army and belonged to the 'Nazi category' made their getaway. It is unknown if this was an opportunist escape or pre-planned. By the Monday evening, they had reached the town of Thurso, where they were noticed due to their German uniforms. They were recaptured at the local cinema accompanied by two young Thurso girls and escorted back to the camp. This was only the beginning.

Within two hours of their arrival back at the camp, they had broken through several locked doors and escaped once more. This time, they took no chances. Hiding in barns, ruined cottages and down by the river that runs from Watten to Thurso, they kept watch for the passing army trucks and ducked and dived whenever necessary.

A full-scale search was launched by Lt.-Col. Murray. Separate groups of guards were mobilised in order to carry out a thorough search of the area, including Polish troops from Castletown, Thurso and Skitten. By the Tuesday morning, the search had covered the district as far as Helmsdale in Sutherland, as one of the escaped men had previously made it that far, but it was to no avail. The guards found no trace of them and returned to camp. Things were to turn round in the evening.

In Thurso a local policeman saw the two young girls who had been seen at the cinema with the men the night before. They were walking up by the Riverside path, carrying a parcel, chatting to each other in hushed voices. It looked suspicious to the policeman and he called into his station. The policeman was advised by his superiors to inform the military authorities and soon a pursuit of the men was under way. The camp guards rushed to Thurso and saw the men with the girls by the iron bridge that spans the Thurso River. The German soldiers saw the camp guards and made a run for it. They hastily scampered up a railway embankment, hotly pursued by the guards. Several shots were fired at the men, but the Germans remained uninjured and finally disappeared into the thick fog that had descended. With the compounded problems of the weather and the darkness falling, the search was called off for the night and the guards returned to Watten.

In the meantime Nohr and Verborg hid in the darkness, surrounded by the thick fog. As the temperature dropped, the colder the two men became. Huddled together on the banks of the river, they tried to get some sleep for they knew their pursuers would return at first light.

The two girls, meanwhile, were taken to Thurso police station and questioned about the prisoners. Terrified by the shooting, they told the police what they knew. The police also had a look in their parcel. Inside was a selection of food and shaving equipment.

The following day the search resumed for Nohr and Verborg but to no avail. It was as if they had disappeared into thin air. The camp guards scoured the area in trucks stopping in every village, asking about the sightings of the men, describing them as being both 5 feet 7 inches tall with dark complexions, with one of them wearing spectacles, but there had been nothing. It did not help that the fog seemed to take its time in clearing the following morning either. The only other hope the guards had at that point was that the men must have been running out of food, but there were no reports of any break-ins. No one was missing any food from their larders and no farmer reported missing goods. Unbeknown to the camp guards, the men were already many miles away.

Overnight Nohr and Verborg had hatched a plan, and using the darkness and fog to their advantage, made their way out of Thurso. They decided they would steal British uniforms and make their way out of the country. For food, the men managed to pilfer some from local houses and farms, plus they still had some the girls had given them earlier. Another source of provisions came from the river. The Thurso River had an abundance of fish including salmon, trout and grilse, and wildfowl.

The two men remained on the run for several more days. Verborg, as it transpired, could speak English well, while his companion could speak only a little, and it is thought this is how they managed to survive for so long. However, on Saturday 23 August, the game was up. Having managed to secure railway tickets and clothing coupons, as well as being dressed in British Army uniforms procured from further up the line, the men had made it as far south as Perth. The tickets were valid for an overnight journey from Inverness to Glasgow but one of the vigilant passengers on board became suspicious. Sergeant-Major Cruickshanks of the Cameron Highlanders was travelling overnight from Inverness to Perth and became more interested in the two men wearing the British battledress. Somehow there was something that did not quite add up about the men. They did not act like British soldiers, and their colouring seemed wrong to him. He concluded that these two men were escaped prisoners of war, but from where he did not know. Instead of approaching them himself, he exited the train at Blair Atholl and got in touch with the London, Midland and Scottish railway control at Perth. When the train arrived in the city, the two men were apprehended and returned to Caithness.

The final escape attempt took place only a few weeks after Nohr and Verborg's one. Rottenführer H. Ruehenbeck of the Waffen-SS managed to flee Watten on 1 September 1947 with one of the camp's own vehicles. The 6 feet tall fair-haired Ruehenbeck had the opportunity to help himself to a motorbike and headed off south. The bike had been left with the keys in the ignition and had a fair amount of fuel in its tank. It was an opportunity not to be missed.

Keeping a watch on the guards, Ruehenbeck spent only a very short space of time making sure no one was paying him any attention. A group of guards stood talking and became distracted. That was the signal. Ruehenbeck jumped on the bike, turned the key and it sprang to life. He twisted the throttle and took off along the B870 towards Mybster and the road south.

The camp's guards were astonished as they watched helplessly while the motorcycle disappeared from view. It had been a major breach of security and they knew that once Murray had been informed they would pay for their mistake. They were right. Two camp guards knocked on his office door and entered. When the camp commandant was told, he was furious. This was the most serious incident the camp had experienced. While escapes were expected, for a British soldier to leave keys in a vehicle that was left unattended long enough for a prisoner to steal it was wholly unacceptable. Murray ordered a manhunt for the prisoner and an investigation over the motorcycle. Never again were vehicles in the compound left with keys in the ignition.

After covering 180 miles, Ruehenbeck abandoned the bike near Dalwhinnie, south of Inverness, when it ran out of fuel. A man fitting his description was sighted walking south in that area, and as his description was flashed all over northern Scotland it was only a matter of time before he was recaptured.

Ruehenbeck managed to hitch lifts and made it down to central Scotland. Under the cover of night, he clambered aboard a ship at Leith and hid, hoping he had eluded the British. Unfortunately for him, he was found and was handed over to the authorities.

On 4 of September the police in Wick made the announcement that Ruehenbeck had been recaptured and the search was called off in Caithness. They told the public that he had been trying to stow away on a ship but had been found and had been sent to Redford Barracks in Edinburgh for safekeeping. He was the last prisoner of war at Camp 165 to escape.

It is significant that all of the escape attempts happened between the months of May and September, with the exception of one in 1946. The weather in Caithness can be unforgiving and it is unlikely that any of the prisoners would have thought about escape whilst the fields were deep in snow or the winds were howling around them. They chose their timing carefully. It was better to stay in the relative safety and warmth of the camp rather than be forced to engage with the winter elements. The only time that would be suitable was during the warmer months, although the light of the days was long and meant timing was everything. Nohr and Verborg were simply lucky that they had fog to shield them to make their getaway, yet even so, when the men were caught, they provided no resistance to returning to the camp. Perhaps it was a case of better to be dry and fed than be on the run, not knowing where you were, looking over your shoulder, awaiting a shot from a farmer's gun.

None the less, the escape attempts did not go unpunished. When the prisoners were recaptured, the rest of the men in their compound suffered for it. In one incident, one of the camp guards, Frank Potter, caught a prisoner, Oberleutnant W. Christ, lurking by the armoury. It was late at night and the ideal time for an escape attempt. However, the young Potter took him to Murray, who was by this time in bed. A German interpreter was called upon and during the questioning Murray had already decided what the man's punishment should be. Christ denied that he was contemplating escape and argued that he was just standing staring out of the camp. Asked why he was doing it so late at night, he fumbled and Murray took that as being the admission of guilt. Murray was so convinced that an escape attempt had been thwarted, he decided on a suitable punishment as a warning to other men in the camp. The cold stone hut that made up the camp's prison became the young German's home for thirty days. He was allowed no visitors except the person delivering his meals to him. That was not to say he did not communicate with the outside world. He could be heard shouting and cursing, his derision for the British clearly audible.

In another incident, in the winter of 1946, a number of soldiers had tried to escape but their plan was foiled. As a punishment, the men were called from their beds in the early hours of the morning, told to dress and were forced to stand in the snow. A few of the prisoners stood merely in their undergarments. They were on the parade ground for some quite considerable time before being allowed to return to their huts, with the exception of the men in their underwear. Shivering with cold, the ones allowed to return to their huts quickly dived into their sleeping bags. The ones left outside stood out longer as a reprimand. By the time they were allowed back inside their huts, their body temperatures had plummeted and were dangerously low. On their return to the huts, the other soldiers had to help them dress and get into their beds. Still, even this kind of punishment did not deter everyone. However, it may have been a factor in decisions made by the soldiers who did try and escape later. If their escape plan failed, and they were caught, May to September was a good time to try – if they were forced to stand outside, they would not freeze.

None of the escape attempts at Camp 165 were on the scale of Devizes, Doonfoot or the infamous Stalag Luft III, at Sagan in Upper Silesia, Poland, in 1944, also known as the Great Escape, yet in their own way they are just as significant. These escape attempts proved that if several factors were in place, including determination, opportunity and careful planning, any prisoner of war camp could be broken out of. The hardest part was not to get caught once the deed was done. And no matter where the camps were, there were serious repercussions.

At the Scottish camp, the repercussions were negligible compared to those meted out by the Germans at Sagan. Not once was a prisoner shot or deliberately killed at the Watten camp because he had tried to escape. The worst that could happen was thirty days of solitary confinement in the detention hut. Perhaps this was where contrasts between countries holding prisoners were at their most divided. In German-occupied Poland, during hostilities, the infamous camp Stalag Luft III held hundreds of British and Allied pilots as prisoners of war. An escape attempt was made on Friday 24 March 1944, and was initially successful, with seventy-six prisoners escaping via a tunnel they had been digging out for months beforehand. Using boards, beds and electric cabling for lighting the tunnel, none of the Luftwaffe guards suspected anything as it was done so discreetly. The tunnel, however, was slightly short and the seventy-seventh man out a day later was spotted and apprehended. The search began for the others. In all, seventy-three prisoners were recaptured within two weeks. Hitler had ordered all of the men to be shot as an example, but eventually, under pressure, he accepted that fifty should be killed.

On a final note on escapes at Watten, one incident stands out simply because it never actually happened. The camp orchestra had been playing locally and had arrived back at the camp late in the evening. The commandant had told them they could lie longer in their bunks in the morning and thanked them for their performances. They headed off to bed.

The following morning, at roll call, the camp guards realised that around twenty or so of the prisoners were missing. A full scale hunt for the men was launched. Within a few minutes, the men were found safe and well in their bunks. Murray had failed to inform the officer due to take the roll call he had given permission for them to miss it because of their engagement the night before.

Chapter 5

The Stutthof Connection

The Hiroshima and Nagasaki bombs wiped out thousands of people to prevent World War II from dragging on any further. The bombings are without a doubt one of the most horrific episodes in twentieth century history. The Japanese government had refused to give up the fight in the Far East, but those two dreadful events forced them to surrender. And so by late August 1945, millions had died all round the world, having fought for their country. It took another six years of diplomacy before World War II was finally over with the signing of two major peace treaties: the first declaring that the state of war between Germany and the United Kingdom was terminated, the second two months later in September 1951 with the Treaty of San Francisco.

Yet for many, not only what they had believed in, but what they were had cost them their lives in another, cataclysmic way because of an unstoppable regime that believed in *Lebensraum* and the Greater German Reich where the German people would reign supreme. Gypsies, homosexuals, the mentally and physically disabled, opponents of the regime, communists and of course Jews from all over Europe ended up in the grisly concentration camps. Thousands of people lost their lives in one particular camp in Poland, near Danzig, that has connections with Watten and the former prisoner of war camp.

In a remote part of occupied Poland, roughly twenty-five miles from Danzig (Gdansk), Stutthof concentration camp was established in September 1939. Originally it was used to hold male civilians who were members of the Polish intelligentsia such as priests, teachers and university graduates. They were seen as political agitators and anti-Nazi. Others included patriotic Poles who simply did not wish Poland to become an annex of a Greater Germany, and men active in the social and economic life of the country. Their activities had been recorded from as early as 1936 and the files opened up as an excuse to arrest them in September 1939. On the first day of the war alone, 1500 Poles were arrested in Danzig and one hundred and fifty of these were sent as the first inmates of Stutthof concentration camp. The camp came under the jurisdiction of the Danzig police chief, but by early 1941, as the women had begun arriving as forced labour, it was handed over to the SS. A year later, it was a fully established concentration camp, built by the internees themselves. The first few hundred prisoners had arrived within days of Poland being invaded, taken from a prison in Danzig. Less than six months later, the camp held over 4000 Polish men.

When the first internees arrived there was little more to the camp than tented accommodation. The first task set to these prisoners was for them to build the camp using the wood from the nearby forest. Early in 1940, barracks, and workshops such as a forge and an electrical workshop, as well as a furniture workshop, had been built. Stables had been erected, as had a slaughterhouse. The camp infirmary had been completed, using one of the barracks, and the camp had its own pharmacy. However, the heads of the camp occupied the most comfortable accommodation which was a rather grand mansion house. Barbed wire surrounded the camp, and around the living accommodation the wire was electrified. Guarding the camp were over 2000 personnel, both men and women. These were not only German nationals, but also Latvians and Ukrainians.

It was following a visit by SS Sturmbannführer Liebenschell in early 1940 that it was suggested to Reichsführer Heinrich Himmler that Stutthof become a concentration camp. Himmler finally agreed to the new status in December 1941 when he wrote that Stutthof was to be taken over as a recognised concentration camp and the order came the following February. It stated that Stutthof was to renamed from simply the SS special camp as it was to Concentration Camp Stutthof. Richard Glücks, the Inspector of Concentration Camps, issued a circular letter stating its new status and announcing SS Sturmbannführer Max Pauly as the camp's commandant. He was the obvious choice as he was already the regional commander of all the internment camps in the area. At this stage the camp had over 4000 internees, almost all of them Polish men.

Heinrich Himmler had visited the camp in December 1941 and suggested the camp be expanded to house more workshops, joineries and metalworking shops. Thus Stutthof expanded holding up to 110,000 men, women and children from all over occupied Europe in its lifetime. The vast majority held in the camp were Polish but there was also a significant number of Lithuanians, some Russians, Germans, Austrians, and even the odd British prisoner. It also held Czechs, Slovaks, White Russians and Danes. Surprisingly, up until 1944, there were very few Jewish prisoners. The original political prisoners slowly began to be released from Stutthof, but many more inmates were sent to Sachsenhausen in April 1940. By the end of the year, there were only just over 1000 inmates. However, after Himmler's order on expansion, a new camp was built to take some 20,000 Soviet prisoners of war. This camp consisted of 30 barracks which not only included accommodation for the prisoners, but also a canteen, kitchen and a quarantine barracks for prisoners arriving with contagious diseases. The men were sent here in July 1943, while the women stayed in what was then termed 'the old camp'. Knowing of the forced labour in the area, it allowed German companies to set up businesses nearby. In April 1944 Commandant Hoppe, Pauly's successor, ordered that the inmates work an eleven hour day with the exception of Sundays which were to be worked only in the mornings. It was, as far as the Germans were concerned, a work camp, and not an extermination camp. Many historians believe that because of the hard labour it was indeed a death camp because so many lost their lives due to overwork and under-nourishment.

Some thirty-nine sub-camps were built coming under the umbrella 'Stutthof'. These sub-camps housed the slave labour for use in local factories. Torun, for example, famous for Copernicus and his scientific revolution, became the labour camp for the German company AEG, and Elblag's slaves went to work for Schinau. Stutthof's own internees were sent to the newly-built factories just outside the main camp. These were DAW, the German Equipment Works, an armaments works, and the Focke-Wulff aeroplane factory, where two new hangers had been built. Others from the camp worked in local brickyards or on farms taken over by the SS, and if they were not allowed out of the camp, they worked in the camp's own workshops.

During their internment the prisoners had to endure horrific conditions. On arrival at the camp, the new inmates noticed was two piles of shoes and combs, saw the familiar sign 'Arbeit Macht Frei', flowers bedecking the balcony and music being played by other prisoners as a greeting. The men and women were told to strip. They were examined, separated out then sent to another room to find camp uniforms. Tattoos came later with their special number that was to remain with them for the rest of their lives and their heads were shaved, although non-Jewish prisoners were allowed to grow back their hair. Malnutrition was widespread. The living conditions were terrible with people sleeping almost on top of each other. The poor sanitation due to lack of washrooms and latrine facilities allowed disease to spread rapidly, causing untold deaths. In these living areas there was absolutely no sanitation. The latrines were open to the air and only a few metres away from the living quarters. If the lack of food and cleanliness caused some deaths, the rest can be put down to executions by way of shoot-ings, hangings, torture, beatings, and to some extent, gassing. A small brick-built gas chamber stood side-by-side with the ovens for burning corpses. A hole in the top of the chamber was used for throwing in the poisonous gas known as Zyklon B. This chamber held over eighty people and it took over half an hour for them to suffocate.

It has been suggested by some historians that the chamber was only ever used when Paul Werner Hoppe was the commandant, between summer and Christmas 1944. Another horrific way of killing off the prisoners was injection. The prisoner would be chosen, perhaps because he had tried to escape or perhaps he had not worked as hard as he should have or perhaps he was just minding his own business. It did not matter. He would then be subjected to some kind of torture, whether physical or mental and finally a needle would be thrust into his heart, containing the drug phenol, also known as carbolic acid, which kills almost instantly. This was originally given intravenously by a medical doctor or his assistant into the arm, but the method changed as it was found to be so much quicker by injecting straight into the heart. The victim would sit in a chair, held down by two inmates while another would cover their eyes so they did not know what was about to happen. Whatever the method, extermination of life within the camp was a daily occurrence.

One particularly brutal man was the head of the Jewish camp, Oberscharführer Foth. Apparently, one day the gas chambers did not work so he simply chose the weakest women from the roll call and murdered them with his own hands by beating them. This was not the only time he did this, nor was he the only one to do it.

Paul Werner Hoppe, the second commandant
of Stutthof concentration camp.

The work regime was hard, and if an inmate was caught trying to escape from the drudgery of it, they were murdered. However, confirmation of the punishment always had to come directly from Berlin before being carried out. In July 1944 Hoppe had issued an order that sufficient work should be performed by the inmate commandos but that the inmates themselves were not be beaten, pushed, or touched as long as they knew what was expected of them. Stutthof, like all other camps, had regulations laid down. To what extent these were ignored is unknown, but without a doubt, they were. The SS guards, for example, were not allowed to carry out corporal punishment without higher authorisation, usually directly from Hoppe or Berlin, yet this was done frequently. The Kapos, prisoners who had been recruited from within the camp to police their fellow inmates and who in return were given privileges, were often even more brutal than the SS guards. Many Kapos were criminals in their civilian life and were more than happy to beat or torture the professionals held at the camp. Yet they were in no man's land. They did not want to be prisoners and if offered the position of Kapo, the women had to accept for fear of reprisals for refusing. Yet neither were they in charge. The SS guards made sure they knew where they came in the pecking order. However, having the power over the ordinary prisoners gave them status and they were greatly feared.

In one incident, a contingent of women arrived at Stutthof only to be met by Kapos.

One of them, a Hungarian, was later to order the women to lie down, threw buckets of water over them and told them not to move until morning. In other incidents, if a prisoner even glanced at a Kapo, and that glance was seen and the Kapo did not like it, he or she would suffer by way of a baton hitting them full force on the head or some form of other physical punishment. The washrooms in Stutthof appear to have been a favourite place for torture. Not all Kapos were like this, but the brutality of the Germans above them had forced many to become as hardened and vicious as their captors. The role of the Kapo was vital to the camp in maintaining discipline and many did their job with great enthusiasm. It was a simple rule. If the SS gave an order to a Kapo, it would be carried out without hesitation or question. Obedience from all sections in the camp was paramount to the smooth running of the facility.

It was in 1942 that SS Hauptsturmführer Pauly was informed that he was to be reassigned and by August, he had moved on to the Neuengamme concentration camp in a southeastern district of Hamburg. It was for the atrocities carried out at Neuengamme that a British court sentenced him to death after the war. The court heard that out of 106,000 prisoners, 55,000 died due to the incredibly hard labour enforced on them and the lack of nutrition and sanitation. The SS guard inflicted horrific beatings on the inmates, no matter what the gender, and death by other means included hangings, shootings and lethal injections. The conditions at the camp were horrendous from the start. Food rations were less than adequate and the inmates were forced to do hard labour in all weathers. Many of the women stopped menstruating due to the malnutrition. Lack of medical supplies, disease and deficiencies in food and sanitation caused countless deaths. During the last weeks of the war, when the Nazis knew the war was lost, they decided to evacuate Neuengamme. On this death march, around 10,000 of the inmates lost their lives. When the British liberated the camp in May 1945, so many of the soldiers who had been to the camp came back to their base sick that others refused to go. They were horror-struck by the situation and could not stomach the sheer inhumanity they had come across. There were people half dead and dying and so hungry their skeleton showed every single bone in their body. Bodies lay strewn in the grounds. Pauly was hanged in Hamelin prison in October 1946 at the age of 39 for his part in Hitler's regime.

After Pauly's promotion to Neuengamme, Stutthof fell into the hands of SS Sturmbannführer Paul Werner Hoppe. He was to serve as its commandant until April 1945.

Hoppe had been born in February 1910 in Berlin, just four years before the outbreak of World War I. His father was an architect, but Hoppe never got the chance to know him. He died when Paul was only two and a half years old. Hoppe was sent away to live with relatives of his mother where he stayed until 1919.

By the end of World War I the German soldiers and civilians alike felt betrayed by their leaders and it was under this cloud that Hitler's rise to power began its stranglehold over the nation. Hoppe grew up hearing the stories of the defeat and the betrayal of those who signed the armistice. The men on the frontline blamed the government, the communists and the Jews for this dreadful misdemeanour.

By the end of 1919 the young Hoppe was sent back to Berlin, to stay with his uncle, who coincidentally was an architect like his father, and aunt. They had no children, but along with Paul, they adopted a little girl, making their family complete. The middle class family life was good. By the mid-1920s the country was enjoying a boom time recovering from the poverty inflicted after the Treaty of Versailles. Paul attended the local gymnasium and passed his exams in 1929, having excelled in mathematics, Latin and sports. With school life behind him, he left Berlin and travelled extensively. He found work as a gardener's assistant and thoroughly enjoyed the outdoor life. This gave him a taste for horticulture, which he followed up in the University of Berlin where he studied horticultural techniques.

By 1933 Hitler had risen to lead the Nationalsozialistische Deutsche Arbeiterpartei or NSDAP, and had become Chancellor. He gave young men like Hoppe hope for the future of a greater Germany with an empire spreading from east to west in revenge for its defeat in 1918. The Treaty of Versailles was being watered down. Hitler's final destruction of the Treaty led to World War II after the re-militarization of the Rhineland in 1936, the Anschluß in Austria in 1938, and finally the expansion east into Poland in 1939. Between 1919 and 1933 the people of Germany fell into two ideological categories and a war of attrition began between the Communists and the Nationalists. Street fighting was commonplace. However, it was the young Adolf Hitler's now legendary oratory that forced more and more Germans to side with him. He spoke of the Bolshevik Jews and of the horrors which had happened in Russia since the fall of the Russian Empire. This was the beginning of the widespread hatred for the Jewish community in Germany. Hitler had linked the two groups into one. Bolshevism and Jews were one and the same. Only he could deal with the problem.

It was at the time of Hitler's victory in becoming Chancellor that Hoppe joined the SS, the Schutszstaffel, or protection squad, at the age of twenty-three. His political ideals had caused great anxiety within his family and finally caused a breakdown in his relationship with his uncle, who he saw as a democrat. Without the financial support from his uncle, and with nowhere to live, Hoppe had to give up his studies. However, after a time away from them, he returned to his studies through a nationalist socialist student's organisation and felt indebted to the organisation for their help. This was when he became more and more involved in the movement. He completed his studies and for a time used them while he worked as a horticultural technician, but his true goal was to become an officer in the SS. Steadily, he rose through the ranks. He visited the SS-Führerschule in Braunschweig and began his ascension. By 1936 he became SS-Untersturmführer and a year later was SS-Obersturmführer. In 1938 the same year as he married the daughter of the camp commandant Hermann Baranowski of Sachsenhausen, he became a Hauptsturmführer.

Baranowski had been in the German navy during World War I and had taken part in the Battle of Jutland. By the end of the war, he was in the IX Minesweeper flotilla but by September 1920, he had left. He worked as a clerk in the Kiel branch of the Bergedorf iron-works briefly, then as an agent for a catering firm in Hamburg, during which time he became a member of the NSDAP. In 1931 he entered the SS and worked his way up the ranks. In 1936 he had become the Führer of 4 SS Standarte at the *Konzentration Lager* (KL) Lichtenburg, of which he later became commandant, then went on to be the protective custody camp leader of Dachau and finally became the camp commandant at Sachsenhausen on 1 March 1938.

He died in 1940 after a long illness. Rumours surrounded his death and it was said his family believed an inmate at Sachsenhausen had poisoned him.

The marriage between Hoppe and Baranowski's daughter was not a happy one by all accounts, and Hoppe spent more and more time with his division and his friends rather than with his wife. However, the marriage did help with his SS career as he became Theodor Eicke's adjutant. Finally, in 1942, he was SS-Sturmbannführer. He had fulfilled his ambitions. He fought in the Russian campaign but in 1942 was seriously wounded in the leg during heavy fighting. Unable to return to lead his company, he took time out to convalesce, then when he had recovered sufficiently was sent to KL Auschwitz, having been promoted once more to command an SS guard detachment there. Hoppe's final posting came in the late summer of 1942. He was sent to head KL Stutthof. He was seen as the ideal candidate and the wound to his leg meant the camp system had reacquired an expert with in-depth knowledge on them.

Hoppe was no stranger to concentration camps. He had been assigned to Dachau as the adjutant of the then camp commandant, and father of the concentration camp movement, SS Gruppenführer Theodor Eicke, and a man whose instructions can be summed up in his camp's motto, 'tolerance means weakness'. One of Eicke's protégés was Rudolf Hoess, who later became commandant of Auschwitz. The main lesson learned from Eicke was how to stir up hatred between the SS guards and the prisoners and that only one thing ever mattered to the soldiers and that was the command given. Furthermore, Hoppe had been involved on Eicke's staff with the inspectorate of concentration camps and also helped in the organisation of the Totenkopfdivision, or SS Death's Head Division. In his SS file there is a reference to him in March 1942. It states: 'As adjutant of SS-Obergruppenführer Eicke, when he was still inspector of the concentration camps, he gained an insight into all questions concerning the concentration camps. For this reason I believe him to be especially suitable for the further use as a camp's commandant … Due to his serious character and the fact that he is free of weakness seems to me especially suitable for the office of a camp's commandant.'

During his time with Eicke, Hoppe had accompanied him during inspections, and although his role was administrative, he saw what was going on. Generally though, he had no direct contact with the atrocities that were unfolding. Eicke and Hoppe had a very strong personal relationship, as their SS files confirm.

Eicke had been born on 17 October 1892, the eleventh child of stationmaster Heinrich Eicke. He dropped out of school at the age of seventeen and joined a Bavarian infantry regiment. In late 1914 he married Bertha Schwebel and they had two children. His son Hermann went on to fight during World War II and lost his life at the age of twenty-one in 1941. During World War I, Eicke won an Iron Cross for bravery. However, after the war, his hatred for the Weimar Republic and its policies grew and having trained as a policeman, he passed his exams but because as such he was not supposed to demonstrate in political marches, he found it incredibly difficult to find employment. In 1923, however, he finally secured a job with IG Farben and became a leader in its intelligence section. In 1928 Eicke joined the NSDAP and became a member of the SA, although he left this roughly eighteen months later so he could join the SS. Heinrich Himmler took note of Eicke and he was promoted to Standartenführer in 1931.

For two years, Eicke lived in Italy due to a bomb plot – which he had devised back in Bavaria against his enemies – and only returned to Germany once Hitler was in power. On 28 June 1933 Eicke became commandant of Dachau concentration camp. As SS Oberführer, he made changes to the camp system. All guards were to obey orders with no questions asked and they were to support Hitler and the SS unconditionally. He impressed Himmler, not only by his stance on loyalty but also his strong views on anti-Semitism and anti-communism. As such he was promoted once more, this time to SS Brigadeführer in January 1934. In the summer of that year, he became the inspector of concentration camps. After a further promotion to SS Gruppenführer, he began his work in earnest. The smaller camps were dismantled and reorganised as larger ones. These consisted of the now infamous camps of Dachau, Sachsenhausen and Buchenwald as well as the building of new camps in Austria and eventually Poland. In his role, it became clear what he was like as a man. He was fearless, cruel and brutal and it was his rigidity towards the callousness that made him a legend with his guards. Never were they to show compassion towards the prisoner but rule with an iron fist no matter what. Also during this time, Eicke had been given the task of forming the SS Totenkopf unit, known as Death's Head units. These were to be part of the Waffen-SS and their main role was to hunt down and kill perceived enemies, such as Jews and Communists as well as homosexuals and gypsies. One group had particular attention at this time and these were former government officials who were still seen as a threat to Hitler's power. Hoppe was one of only a select few who helped Eicke with the organisation of those units.

At the outbreak of World War II, Eicke was given command of SS Division Totenkopf and it is believed that his murderous nature was involved in the massacre of British prisoners of war at Le Paradis in 1940 as well as the execution of Soviet officers. In 1941, he was severely injured by a mine blast. However, in February 1943, shortly after he was promoted to SS Obergruppenführer, Eicke was killed on the Eastern Front when his Storch aircraft was shot down during fighting at the Third Battle of Kharkov. Hoppe was said to be devastated on hearing this news but the propaganda machine went into full swing. When the news filtered through to the public, they were told he had died a hero's death, fighting against the Bolsheviks.

Meanwhile Hoppe had taken over as commandant of Stutthof on 1 September 1942 and remained there until April 1945. As the war wore on, conditions inside the camp worsened. Overcrowding was the main problem but so was disease. Typhus, dysentery, diphtheria and scarlet fever were rampant. In 1942, a typhus epidemic killed hundreds of prisoners. Hospital facilities were hurriedly expanded but due to lack of medicines and equipment very little could be done. This, compounded by winter conditions and poor sanitation, merely made an already beleaguered camp worse. It was during the winter of 1944–5 that the camp suffered its worst epidemic. Typhus, also known as prison fever for its voracity in spreading in crowded, unhygienic conditions, spread through the camp at an astonishing rate. The human body louse passes it on, causing fever, headache, exhaustion and a rash, and in the camp it was certainly easily transmitted from person to person. It is perhaps his actions here that make historians re-think the brutality of the camp. Some had suggested that the outbreak was deliberate as way of killing off the inmates, yet if that was the case, Hoppe condemned his own men to death. In his decree on 29 December 1944 he announced that the 'entry and leaving of the new women's camps I, II and III is blocked, effective immediately, due to the contagion of typhus'. It is clear that this step was taken to minimise causalities. He was no fool. The local factories needed workers. Without them, they would run dry. It is clear that the policy of Stutthof was not to use it as a concentration camp like Auschwitz, Buchenwald or Dachau. This aside, all camp commandants had received orders in 1943 that inmates were to be kept as healthy as possible to work in the factories while the German labour force went off to fight for their country. Their role in the Greater German Reich was absolutely necessary.

However, this not withstanding, Hoppe had indeed received orders to kill the unfit men and women who arrived at the camp. Under camp regulations, it had already been approved that if the sick, infirm and disabled came to any of the concentrations camps, they were to be gassed. During the Third Reich, in some cases, this was seen as euthanasia. One account recalls some Russians arriving at the camps who were blind, or missing a limb and starving. These soldiers had been held as prisoners of war at a different camp and were transported to Stutthof in August 1944. For three days and nights they remained out in the open with no shelter and no food while decisions were made as to what to do with them. Their clothes were ragged and they were exhausted. It is claimed that Hoppe thought these individuals were not worth feeding and having discussed it with the protective custody leader Theodor Meyer, and Reporter Leader Arno Chemnitz, they were eventually gassed later that day. Meyer was responsible for roll calls twice daily in order to establish the manpower available. He was also responsible for separating the Jews from, for example, the Russians or Germans. Hoppe may have seen this as euthanasia, but in reality they were simply unfit for work and of no use to the local businesses. If Hoppe had spared them, he would have the burden of feeding them, clothing them and so on. It was not an option for Hoppe.

The camp no longer accepted men by the late autumn of 1944. They were separated from the women and children and sent to other camps such as Dachau. One woman held at Stutthof in 1944 for a time was the artist Esther Lurie. She had been born in Latvia in 1913 and by the time World War II broke, she was a renowned artist. Whilst in Lithuania, she was captured by the Nazis and held at Kovno Ghetto where she began drawing her new world. She continued this when she ended up at Stutthof in 1944. Here she was asked by the prisoners to draw them. In return, using the age-old bartering system, she agreed. Her price was food. She managed to get hold of paper and pencils from a young girl working in the camp and drew sketches for the women. She also drew pictures for herself. For the five months she was at Stutthof she hid these drawings in her clothing.

Another way of surviving for the women in the camp was sex. Some of the women were sent to work in the camp's offices and here they were able to interact with their captors. Using the one thing they could, they had sex in return for extra food. These women tended to be non-Jewish. In return for extra bread, a potato or an apple, they slept with their enemy in order to survive. Whether they slept with the Kapos or with the higher ranks of the SS, it did not matter. It was a means to an end. The problem only arose when the women discovered they were pregnant. Many tried to abort in any way they could but if nothing worked, they took their own lives rather than be sent to the gas chamber.

This age-old bartering also went on at the camp's fence. By a cruel twist of fate, the camp was surrounded by potato fields and often the people working them were only wearing ragged pre-war clothing. In return for some potatoes, the prisoners would give these workers anything they could from scarves to jewellery acquired by sometimes devious but life-saving means. Other food stuffs were also to be had in this way such as an egg or some butter, but it had to remain hidden until it was safe, for if they were found to have any extra rations they would suffer at the hands of the Kapos. As far as the Kapos were concerned, the prisoners had their rations and that was it. Otherwise, the Kapos would have felt as if they were losing out.

The camp was liberated, without Hoppe seeing it, on 9 May 1945. Between its inception and its liberation by the Russians, it is thought that around 65,000 people lost their lives at Stutthof. On 25 January that year, with gunfire only a few miles away, Hoppe called for evacuation of the camp. Thousands of mainly Jews were forced to march west, many of them dying en route not only due to the harsh winter conditions and lack of shelter but lack of food and the deprivation of sleep and rest. If the prisoners brought attention to themselves by walking too slowly and showing they were weak, they were shot. Others were suffering from the effects of typhus and so were susceptible to pneumonia. It was said that 5000 prisoners from the smaller sub-camps of Stutthof were marched up to the Baltic coast and forced into the freezing water where they gunned down by Ukrainian guards. In one incident, a group of the prisoners were led into a barn where they huddled together for warmth. The guards closed the doors and set it alight. Very few escaped. In April, those who remained at the camp were shipped out but like the incident in January, many were forced into the sea and shot. Those who survived were sent in a flotilla of boats to other concentration camps, mainly to Neuengamme. It was estimated that out of the original 50,000 who had been evacuated from the camp, half had lost their lives. However, not everyone left the camp. The ill stayed and awaited their fate as the Russians advanced, as did a small group who were to oversee the camp's closure. After the Red Army liberated the camp, investigations of the crimes committed there began immediately.

Hoppe was captured by the British and arrested towards the end of hostilities, and finally reached Camp 165 at Watten. He is recorded as being in Caithness between August 1947 and January 1948, just prior to the closure of the camp. After screening, he was politically graded 'C+' due to his position at Stutthof.

The political screening process at Watten was approached carefully. Many of the prisoners who arrived were hostile and suspicious at first because of the way they had been treated in other camps during a similar type of process. Watten took the view of gaining trust by simply not showing any hostility towards the captured men. Hoppe, although seen as a hard core Nazi, was treated in exactly the same way as the other men being screened, although the younger men's attitudes were a worry. With no wife or children to bring stability, these younger men were deemed 'genuine' fanatics according to a letter dated 25 September 1947 and were 'capable of any folly'. This 'pathological obsession' with fanaticism had already 'reached one small group at Watten'. However, Hoppe seems to have kept his head down and caused no trouble at the camp.

Hoppe was transferred from Watten to London for interrogation between late September and early October to the LDC. The head of the Cage was Lt.-Col. Alexander Scotland, a man in his sixties who had spent time in the German army and spoke the language fluently. Whether he personally interrogated Hoppe is unclear, but whatever the outcome, Hoppe was returned north to the camp.

He is recorded in Camp 165 during a visit from Major Bieri of the International Committee of the Red Cross in August 1947. On a return visit to the camp on 31 December 1947, Bieri comments on Hoppe thus: 'The Concentration Camp Commandant Hoppe (whom I saw during my last visit) ... will on recovery, be handed over to the Polish Government for trial'. According to the same report, his deputy, Theodor Meyer, the Protective Custody Leader at Stutthof, had already been executed, having been found guilty by the Polish Special Criminal Court after his trial in January of that year. However, according to a letter dated 10 December 1947 from the Repatriation Desk in London, a different approach is taken. The letter stated that Hoppe was 'a member of a criminal organisation and will be transferred to Germany for trial'. Obviously, both countries wanted Hoppe to stand trial but only one would succeed.

Somehow though, Hoppe escaped from British custody. He was transported to Germany on 18 May 1948 to the British internment camp at Fallingbostel, some eighty-five kilometres from Hamburg on the road which leads to Bremen in Lower Saxony, but on 9 June, he escaped. At first he stayed in Germany under the assumed name Werner Salchow, but ended going to Switzerland on 3 October where he entered illegally and worked as a landscape gardener. He lived in Switzerland for two years before returning to his native Germany in December 1952. On his return, he reverted back to his own name thinking that the new Germany would not be interested in him or his role during the war. West German Police finally arrested him five months later in 1953 at Witten. He stood trial at Bochum in North Rhine-Westphalia in 1955. The charge against him was that he was an accessory to murder and involved in the deaths of hundreds of prisoners who had been gassed in the delousing barracks, and the shooting of prisoners in the back of the neck in a room in cold blood. In particular the court mentioned the brutality of killing the pregnant women, mothers with young children, and the sick and infirm. He was initially sentenced to five years and three months imprisonment but on review this was increased to nine years and he eventually served seven and a half years. He had argued that he had merely been following the orders of Hitler and Himmler and that if he had refused to do as he was told, he would have been executed and his family sent to the concentration camps. He also argued that he was too young to understand what was happening. The court dismissed all of his excuses, even though he did show some regret over what he had done at Stutthof. Until the very end, he continued to argue that he had merely been doing his duty under the national socialist system.

Upon his release, he returned to his normal family life with his wife and two children. He became an employee in an insurance firm in Bochum and was devoted to his children. He is known to have spoken at length on World War II, but never did he talk about his time in Poland.

Just a few months before his death, Hoppe became paranoid. His thoughts turned more and more to the crimes committed at Stutthof, and he began to feel threatened by an invisible group of conspirators, including his eldest son. He thought that the Polish state was hunting him and were going to abduct him in order to take him back to the 'Ostblok', or Eastern Bloc, to stand trial once more. He accused his son of being an agent for the state of Israel and thought that he was about to be kidnapped and hanged in Jerusalem. His paranoia was unjustified. Paul Werner Hoppe died in 1974.

Immediately after the war, the Polish authorities began to collect evidence of the atrocities carried out at Stutthof following the capture of some of the guards and the interviewing of former inmates. Antoni Zachariasziewicz headed the investigation and called on the British, American and French to extradite any former SS members they held. The first court cases were heard between April and June 1946 in the Special Penal Court in Gdansk. Ten people, all of whom were inmates and had collaborated with their Nazi guards, were sentenced to be hanged, which was done in public on 4 July 1946. The next round of cases was heard in October 1947 against twenty-four SS men, including Theodor Meyer. He and eight others were sentenced to death and all were executed. There were two other court cases in November 1947 where thirty-nine SS men were put on trial. As already noted, SS Sturmbannführer Max Pauly was tried in Hamburg for his atrocities at Neuengamme. He was never tried over his alleged crimes in Poland.

As for others brought to trial over Stutthof, these included SS Unterscharführer Otto Knott, a medical officer who had, it was alleged, murdered prisoners in the gas chambers. He had undergone special training for his role in the death chambers, having spent time in other concentration camps. It has been suggested that it was Knott who poured the Zyklon B into the gas chamber at Stutthof, killing up to 3000 inmates this way. The camp's head doctor, Hauptsturmführer Otto Heidl, like Hoppe and Knott, was to be tried at Bochum, but committed suicide in his prison cell. He had served at Stutthof for three years from 1942, having had a spell at Auschwitz. The charge against him was simply the ill treatment of prisoners. He had been present at all the executions, whether gas chamber, hanging or shooting, and he was also on hand during the beatings. In all seventy-two SS personnel were brought to trial. Out of 2000 SS guards at Stutthof this is a tiny number. Consequently many escaped justice.

To this day, historians haggle over the camp. Some believe it was a work camp with a labour reserve for local factories in order to aid the German war effort, while others see it simply as another Auschwitz or Dachau. What can be determined was that people were incarcerated there simply due to their beliefs. The first inmates, the Poles, were sent there due to their anti-Nazi beliefs and because they were members of the intelligentsia, a dangerous combination in an occupied country. Women and children, on arrival at the camp were separated from their husbands and fathers, and some of these women and children were sent on to Auschwitz or Mauthausen where they were executed in the gas chambers. The transport of these people may have been for the influx of a healthier workforce, but Hoppe knew that by sending them to these camps their chances of survival were negligible. After all, he had been involved at their inception. A few historians even go as far as saying that the women and children were sent out together on humanitarian grounds so that they were not separated.

This is a view not shared by many. Many men were worked to death, as were some women, and there is evidence to support the beatings, shootings, hangings, gassings and torture that took place at Stutthof.

Paul Werner Hoppe did indeed believe that he had done his duty for Adolf Hitler and it is a belief he took to the grave with him. What questions were asked of him while he was at Watten is unknown but it was in London where his real questioning would have taken place in the rooms in Kensington. Perhaps history will one day give up the secrets of the interrogation endured by Hoppe in the United Kingdom, but for now the former commandant of Stutthof has a connection with Watten in Scotland that is part of Camp 165's history.

Chapter 6

Das Schwarze Korps and Der Wattener

By the autumn of 1947 the newspaper editor and SS-Obergruppenführer Gunter d'Alquen had arrived at Camp 165 and had become camp leader of Compound O.

Gunter d'Alquen had been born in Essen in October 1910, son of a Protestant merchant named Carl Emil and his wife Julia Rottman. Essen lies in the North Rhine-Westphalia region of Germany, north-east of Düsseldorf in the Ruhr. After finishing secondary school, and having been a member of the Hitler Youth, which he joined in 1926, he joined the NSDAP, the Nationalsozialistische Deutsche Arbeiterpartei, the National Socialist Workers Party in August 1927 and became a Hitler Youth leader for four years. In 1926 he also became a member of the SA, the Sturmabteilung, also known as the Brown Shirts or stormtroopers. He joined the SS on 10 April 1931.

In 1923 the French occupied the Ruhr. Germany had been faltering with her reparations payments so both French and Belgian troops were sent there simply to seize the coal and iron industries so vital to the area's economy and bring Germany to her knees. However, the troops were forced to withdraw in 1925. D'Alquen had known of this occupation and it had a profound effect on him. The Hitler Youth provided just what the young patriotic boys of Germany were looking for. Boys between the ages of 14 and 18 joined and were given strict military-like training, which on the whole took precedence over academic studies. The new Aryan Super Race was being born. At the Hitler-Jugend Camps the boys were taught military discipline and how to use weapons and devise strategies in the event of war. All the boys were issued with uniforms and given ranks and insignia. One of the main aims was the indoctrination of anti-Semitism. This started very early on in the organisation. Jews, communists and homosexuals to name but a few were often seen as being 'Untermensch' or sub-human. These 'parasites' as Hitler would later call them had to be dealt with and this later became the Holocaust. He blamed the Jews for the betrayal as he saw it in 1918 and believed that all German-speaking people should be united as one as long as they had pure German blood. This unification of German speakers stemmed from the Treaty of Versailles

Gunder d'Alquen at his desk.
(Courtesy of: Ingo d'Alquen.)

when Germany lost so much land under its terms and conditions but more than that, he mistakenly believed the Jews were all Communists after a rising in Germany in the 1920s in which coincidentally most of the German Communist Party leaders were Jewish. Bullying by the older members of the Hitler Youth was tolerated to a certain extent in order to weed out the weaker boys who would not be of any use in a future supreme Germany. Being a member of the Youth opened doors and a boy could enter into the SA or SS if he was good enough and showed enough physical, mental and emotion strength.

D'Alquen had gone on to university but never finished his studies, choosing instead to follow his career path into journalism and worked on the *Bremer Zeitung*, a National Socialist newspaper. In 1932 he joined the staff at the newspaper *Volkischer Beobachter* and became its political editor.

The *Volkischer* had been established in 1920 and was the voice at that time of the NSDAP, which had bought it that year. It was hailed as the fighting paper of the Nationalist Socialist movement for a greater Germany and as such its circulation slowly increased from a mere 8000 at its inception to well over one million by 1944. In a 1933 edition, a book-burning incident took place in Berlin and it reported on a speech made by Dr Josef Goebbels. He had said that an overly refined Jewish intellectualism had come to an end and claimed that because of the capitulation of Germany in November 1918, the Jews had filled the libraries with filth and rubbish written by Jewish intellectuals. He spoke of how the German Revolution had made the roads clear again for the emergence of the German character and a pile of Jewish books burned, which the newspaper claimed was poisoned literature. The paper saw it as a German struggle that had just begun against the un-German spirit. Later, in November 1938 Goebbels was to write an article for the newspaper on Kristallnacht, whereby he stated the patience of the German people had been exhausted. A German Jew had shot dead Ernst vom Rath, a German diplomat in Paris after he refused to help the young man's family back in Germany who were being force marched to a concentration camp in Poland under vom Rath's orders. It was the excuse the authorities had been waiting for to wreak havoc on the Jewish community. On 9 and 10 November 1938, Jewish homes, businesses and synagogues were destroyed. The state police, dressed in civilian clothes, took sledgehammers and axes and smashed their way along the streets. The shattered glass from the windows covered the pavements. Thousands of synagogues were destroyed all over Germany, Jewish cemeteries were desecrated, and shops and homes were ransacked. Jews were beaten to death in the street while others were forced to watch. Over 30,000 men were transported to concentration camps. The Jewish community was forced to pay for the damage and pay compensation for the death of vom Rath. Insurance for their property was not to be paid to them but to the Government because of the damage done to the German nation. After Kristallnacht, many Jews decided to emigrate. Many of the German civilians took part in the riots simply because they were caught up by the secret police in their actions.

Shortly after Kristallnacht, Hermann Göring received a letter from Hitler requesting that the Jewish Question be sorted one way or the other. It was the beginning of the end for the Jews in Germany. At a conference at the Ministry of Aviation that same month, of around one hundred officials including Göring and Goebbels, it was decided that all businesses in Germany were to be Aryan-run and that Jews would be refused entry to certain buildings or events, including public swimming pools and the theatres. The unanimous verdict was that no matter what, Germany was to be rid of the Jews in any way possible. By 1939, Berlin had seen a massive rise in the number of Jewish families wishing to emigrate, from 40,000 in 1938 to 78,000 in 1939. Life was becoming intolerable for them.

In one of its last editions, in April 1945, the *Volkischer* hailed Hitler as 'the man of the century' on the occasion of his fifty-sixth birthday. It stated that Germany stayed 'Steadfast and True to the Führer'.

The year 1932 saw d'Alquen also become special correspondent in that area for the local leaders. On 1 October, he became an SS-Sturmführer. It was not long before the young d'Alquen had caught the attention of Heinrich Himmler, who edged him towards *Das Schwarze Korps*, the mouthpiece for the Third Reich regime.

Heinrich Himmler had been born in Munich, Bavaria, in 1900. After leaving school in 1918 he joined a Bavarian regiment but just as they were about to go off and fight, the war was declared over so he never saw action. He went on to university and it was while he

Gunter d'Alquen with Hitler.
(Courtesy of: Ingo d'Alquen.)

was studying there that he joined the *Freikorps*, a group of ex-army men disenchanted by German's surrender. By 1927 he had joined the SS. In 1929 he was appointed to lead the SS, the membership of which was less than 300 and seen as like a battalion of the SA, or Sturmabteilung.

By 1933 Himmler was a Gruppenführer and decided to separate the SS from the SA. This was when the SA got the nickname 'Brownshirt', for the SS uniform was black. For his work he was rewarded with the rank of SS-Obergruppenführer und Reichsführer-SS. He was now on an equal footing with the SA commanders, and, at this time, loathed by them, for the SS held the power. A plot was hatched to take out the SA's leader Ernst Röhm and thus demoralise the SA and destroy it. It took some persuasion for Hitler to agree to the plot, for Röhm had been one of the first members of the Nazi Party and had taken part in the Beer Hall Putsch in the 1920s, but agree he did, having had talks with Himmler and Hermann Göring – who went on to become commander of the Luftwaffe. These two were given the task of overseeing the killing and along with a number of others ordered the execution. Paul Werner Hoppe's future boss, Theodor Eicke, eventually carried out the task after what was to become known as the Night of the Long Knives on 30 June 1934. That night, many top officials in the SA were murdered and all together it is thought around 400 people lost their lives, although officially the number stood at less than 100. Hitler's meteoric rise to absolute power was complete. Röhm was taken to Stadelheim Prison in Munich and offered a gun with a single bullet in it so he could take his own life. He declined, so on 2 July Eicke did it for him on the orders of SS-Obergruppenführer Josef 'Sepp' Dietrich. It was around this time that Himmler's views, and those of Hitler, became apparent, and so began the formation of the idea of a concentration camp system and the SD – Sicherheitdienst or the intelligence section of the SS – began to seek out Jews, gypsies, communists, and homosexuals, as well as those who did not share the Nazi view of the world. Himmler opened the camp at Dachau in March 1933. With this as his background, Heinrich Himmler could see the possibilities in the writings of the young d'Alquen and knew how to utilise this to its full potential.

In March 1935 d'Alquen was appointed *Das Schwarze Korps*'s editor. By this time he had risen through the ranks. He had been promoted to SS-Obersturmführer in November 1933, then the following June to SS-Hauptsturmführer and, by 1935, he was SS-Sturmbannführer.

Under Himmler's direction, *Das Schwarze Korps* became the voice of Himmler. D'Alquen published articles that attacked those who criticised the regime. Among them were intellectuals, scientists and business leaders who disagreed with the policies of Hitler. The newspaper was first and foremost, however, anti-Semitic. Numerous articles appeared destroying the credence of the Jewish population within German borders. In an article published in late November 1938, written by Reinhard Heydrich, the true-blooded Germans were encouraged to chase Jews from their homes and isolate them together in a single area where they would have 'as little contact as possible with Germans'. The article describes them as parasites and describes how they would sink into poverty and turn to Bolshevism as their liberator. Communism placed fear into the heart of central Europe and its borders were closely monitored so that it was stopped from spreading west. What is striking about the article is that on the one hand the authorities want to segregate the Jews but by the end, it speaks of them being sub-human and how the German people need to wipe out this new breed 'with fire and sword'. It is a distinct call for the German people to rid the country in any way possible of its Jewish citizens. It calls on the people of Germany not to tolerate the hundreds of thousands of so-called 'criminals within its borders' and said that the Jews intended to wreak havoc on German life. The article ends that the final result would be end of the Jews in Germany. These Jewish citizens 'would be annihilated without trace'. What is apparent is the propaganda entwined in the article. By reading it many Germans may have believed every word written, that the Jews were indeed sub-human and that they all advocated Communism. It appears to have been an early call to arms against the Jews.

During World War II *Das Schwarze Korps* became even stronger in the propaganda stakes. It was used to boost German morale at home and many of the articles were subjected to a rose-coloured picture of what was happening on the front lines. It concentrated on German victories and avoided mentioning any defeat at the hands of the Allies. Satirical cartoons appeared regularly. In one such cartoon, the British were waiting for the inevitable invasion but it claimed the invasion had already taken place, by the Americans. In another, the British were derided after their invasion of Normandy. The cartoon showed the bombing of France as the Allies forced their way inland and a school being hit by shells. In this way, it was hoped the Germans back home would think the British were foolish, killing their own allies, whereas in reality the German forces were retreating and suffering heavy loses and France was being freed. In an article written in 1944 about the dangers of Americanism, the newspaper refers to the Copernican revolution, when Copernicus went against the received wisdom of the church and changed the worldview to a heliocentric world, rather than a geocentric one. He had had the spirit to say what he truly believed and wrote his theory in his book *De Revolutionibus Orbium Coelsetium* in the mid-sixteenth century. This analogy was used to show the German people that the past dogmas and the rise of science was a victory of youth and the young had always been the staging post that helped bring the ideas of nationalism to fruition. The Hitler Youth in particular were the new movement, which was building up and maintaining cultural idealism and were seen as the hope for the future of the true German bloodline – this would make the young Germany the greatest power on earth. America was seen as an old country with dying liberalism, which was under the control of Jews. Germany in contrast was seen as a young nation, and ready to topple old regimes, including America. Yet by this time Adolf Hitler knew the war was lost. He was just unwilling to accept defeat and tell his people it was futile to carry on fighting. If he had, many German lives might have been saved.

It was during the war that d'Alquen became a distinguished reporter for the newspaper. Himmler rewarded d'Alquen by appointing him head of the Wehrmacht propaganda machine towards the end of the war, hoping to buoy up both the troops on the fronts and the civilians back home. Himmler and d'Alquen had a fairly good relationship. They met on numerous occasions, both on official business and more informally. When d'Alquen married the beautiful Erika Schrader in 1935, Heinrich Himmler was one of the witnesses. A photograph exists of the happy couple, immediately after their marriage, and in the background Himmler is smiling and chatting to another man, thought to be SA-Standartenführer Landesrat Dr Hans Joachim Apffelstaedt. Erica was three years younger than her husband and by the time the marriage had taken place the couple already had a daughter, Heide. They went on to have three more children – Wolf, Klaus and Till.

D'Alquen was a member of the elite ranks. Later d'Alquen was to write that Himmler had influenced his own views, especially with regard to breeding and selection. He also understood Himmler's metaphors with regard to the Jews, such as calling for the extermination of the 'vermin', and his stance on homosexuals, who were to be eliminated 'root and branch'.

When Poland fell in September 1939, Himmler was again to refer to his university education in agronomy, by saying that he was standing on German soil once more, a reference to when Germany lost land to Poland under Versailles and referred to the Jews and other unwanted groups as 'vermin' who could be controlled by the German hawks.

In 1939 d'Alquen published the official history of the SS in his book *Die SS, Gesichte, Aufgabe und Organiztion der Schutzstaffeln der NSDAP* which was basically a history of the organisation. In it, d'Alquen wrote of how Adolf Hitler appointed Heinrich Himmler Reichsfuhrer SS and how he assumed charge of the entire 280 men of the Schutzstaffel. Hitler had charged Himmler with forming the organisation into an elite group which was to be faithful and steadfast in any and every situation. D'Alquen saw this day as the very first day of the SS. He goes on to write that on the day Hitler took power there were 52,000 SS men. By 1939 and the eve of war, this had more than quadrupled to over 240,000 members. All members were screened. They had to be the cream of the crop physically and demonstrate their dependability and faithfulness before they were accepted. He wrote that this general SS stood fully and wholly on call with its fourteen corps, thirty-eight divisions, over one hundred infantry regiments, nineteen mounted regiments, fourteen communication battalions, and nine engineer battalions, as well as motorised and medical units. Originally, the SS had been set up as a protective force to look after the security of Hitler but now, under his leadership, they were in charge of Germany.

In order to become a member of the SS certain procedures were followed. Having been confirmed for his SS suitability and SS merit, the Hitler Youth candidate, on reaching the age of 18, would then become an SS applicant. He was handed over to the SS as an SS candidate on the Reichsparteitag in the same year that he was presented with his SS certificate. Following this, and after a brief probationary period, he would then swear his oath to the Führer.

The SS candidate was then to go on and earn his army sport badge and the bronze Reich sport badge. After achieving that, he would go into the Labour service or Arbeitsdienst, and finally to the Wehrmacht at the age of nineteen, depending on when his birthday fell. He was to spend two years with the Wehrmacht but in order to further his career he would have to do additional training. In the time that remained before his final acceptance into the SS, the young man would have to undertake training and education regarding the SS ideologically when he would learn about what he could and could not do, with a firm emphasis on the choice of future wife as well as learning about the honours instilled within SS rule. It would only be on completion of this part of his training that the man would enter into a life with the SS.

On the day the candidate entered the SS, 9 November, he was given the right to wear the SS dagger and he had to promise that he would uphold the basic laws of the SS at all times. He had to pledge that he would defend the honour laws of the SS as stated in the SS code and he would become a full member of *Das Schwarze Korps*, the Black Corps. In the Oath of the SS Man the new recruit had to swear steadfast loyalty to Adolf Hitler and swore obedience to those Hitler had named to command him until he died. It was blind allegiance.

D'Alquen wrote that the newly-appointed SS man would remain in active service as a general SS man until he reached the age of thirty-five when he would then be transferred, if he requested, to the SS Reserve. When he reached the age of forty-five he was then to trans-fer into an SS inactive corps. He stated that the National Socialists were firmly convinced of the ideology that the overall objective of the SS and Germany as a whole was that only good blood would produce the best human race. There was to be no deviation from this pure blood whatsoever.

As mentioned, *Die SS* also set down the strict rules that were to be applied before any marriage could take place. In the Race and Settlement Agency the marriage applications of the SS men were to be handled in the Relations Office. This was because no SS man could openly marry without the permission of the Reichsführer SS under the conditions of the marriage law of 1931. It meant that a medical examination was required for man and his future wife. The future wife had to prove her worth by stating her ideology and proving that her blood-line was pure and of German ancestry. Furthermore, the family tree was required of both the man and the woman, especially for the officers who wished to marry, back to 1750, and for non-commissioned officers, back to 1800. The law also required them to produce a copy of the hereditary health certificate. The German children of the future were to be pure just like their parents, grandparents and great grandparents alike. No foreign blood, especially Jewish blood, was tolerable in Hitler's regime.

D'Alquen's other works included *Das ist der Sieg*, of which at least 120,000 copies were produced, and *Waffen-SS im Westen* in 1941. For the first publication, d'Alquen had asked the people of Germany to write what they thought of Adolf Hitler and what he meant to them. D'Alquen's introduction is quite remarkable. It is clear that the letters he had received had spoken highly of the Führer and he was delighted with them. He wrote that Hitler was a combination of force and supremacy and a man totally devoted to Germany. He goes on to say that if the people could stand up in unison, they would all speak of Hitler as a great leader. There is an emphasis on blood in the article too. He wrote that those who were not of pure German blood could never understand the Führer or his people. He believed this caused the problem and led those of impure blood to seek a war against them. The introduction continued with what had been required in the letters, by suggesting the people compare Hitler to their father or brother. His outlook was that the Führer belonged to everyone. The article was full of adoration for the leader, including references to him holding the hands of the people and that his orders were merely a reflection of what the Germans wanted to happen anyway. Also, it refers to those who have lost their lives during battle, whether in the air, on land or at sea and suggested that when they were dying their last words were of the Führer. It is an astonishing piece of prose.

In January 1940 a Waffen-SS war reporting company was established. Platoons were attached so they could write about the war on the western front. In the spring of 1941, during the Balkans campaign, they expanded due to the different parts of Europe where fighting was taking place. By December 1943 the reporters' unit was large enough to hold the title of being of regimental size and took the honorary title of SS-Standarte Kurt Eggers, named after the former editor of *Das Schwarze Korps*.

Eggers had published many articles, books and plays during his career, including *Von der Freiheit des Kriegers* in 1940, which is a dialogue between two soldiers on the Eastern Front from a Nazi point of view. Eggers had been born in 1905, the son of a banker. Eventually he became a member of Goebbels' poet circle and began writing songs for soldiers to sing. Many of his books, poems and plays were influenced by Ulrich of Hutten, a late fifteenth-century critic of the Catholic Church. Hutten, a follower of Martin Luther, the German Reformationist, had tried to start a popular crusade against the church and attacked the Archbishop of Trier, but the Archbishop held out and Hutten died in 1523, having written a book on syphilis, of which he was dying. Why Eggers may have liked Hutten's work was simply due to his following of Lutheranism. Luther had published a pamphlet in 1543, *Von den Juden und ihre Lügen*, ['On the Jews and their Lies'], which called for synagogues to be set alight, Jewish prayer books to be destroyed, the destruction of Jewish homes and forbidding rabbis to teach. This pamphlet was given to the editor of the Nazi newspaper *Der Stürmer* and sounds eerily like the destruction of the Jews in 1940s Germany. Yet this pamphlet, calling for Jews to be forced into labour or expelled for all time and calling them venomous worms was written four centuries before. The newspaper later described the pamphlet as quintessentially contemporary. Eggers himself was killed in action whilst serving with the 5th SS-Division in August 1943 near Kharkov in Russia.

The soldiers enlisted in the SS-Standarte Kurt Eggers were all volunteers who had experience of writing and were politically motivated, although there were sub-units which dealt with other matters of journalism such as photography and the filming of battles. The staff processed the material coming in from the front lines, edited it and sent it out when it was ready. Many could speak different languages and amongst the recruits were Americans and one British man as well as a New Zealander. One other member of note is d'Alquen's brother. Rolf d'Alquen shared the views of his elder brother and also joined the SS-Standarte Kurt Eggers, reporting on the battles being fought. In 1931, at the age of nineteen, Rolf joined the NSDAP and became a member of the SS. He, like Gunter, worked on *Das Schwarze Korps* and had risen in the SS ranks. Rolf died in 1993 at the age of 80.

Over the course of the war, many journalists served with different detachments. Training had taken place at Berlin-Zehlendorf and it was there that the decision was made as to where the newly-trained recruit would serve. D'Alquen commanded the SS-Kriegsberichter unit during its existence, from its inception until its disbandment, and was gradually propelled up the ranks, starting out with Waffen-SS Hauptsturmführer der Reserve rising to Standartenführer der Reserve. On 21 December 1944 he was awarded the German Cross in Silver and ended the war as chief of the propaganda department in the OKW (Oberkommando der Wehrmacht), the German High Command. This is not to be confused with the German Army High Command, the OKH. Hitler favoured the former. The OKW was headed by Generalfeldmarschall Wilhelm Keitel, who reported directly to Adolf Hitler. Keitel was eventually hanged by the Allies following the Nuremberg Trials in 1946 aged 64.

D'Alquen, on the other hand, was captured in northern Italy in May 1945 and eventually was transferred to Camp 165 in Watten.

During his incarceration, d'Alquen was not permitted to write home to his family. According to his son Ingo, his wife and children had no idea where he was and he later spoke of how he was interrogated frequently by the Allied secret services. D'Alquen also said that his time in captivity was the worst period in his life. He had become very ill at one point and was not treated the way he thought he ought to have been, although if that was during his time in Watten, there is no record of it.

Camp life proved productive in one way for d'Alquen however. At Watten a few of the internees began a monthly magazine, which was eventually to come under his leadership, known as *Der Wattener*. This not only helped pass the time but also gave the men purpose. The men involved had been journalists just like him, or were good writers, and together they made a formidable team, producing reading material for the other prisoners on varying topics.

As Lagerleiter, or Camp Leader, of Compound O, he interacted with the camp guards on a daily basis. One of the guards at the camp became friendly with d'Alquen, a friendship that lasted until his death. John Acheson, who was later to become a banker in London, was stationed at Watten at the time. He died in 2001.

After Camp 165 closed, d'Alquen was shipped off to the United States, although it was originally thought he would be returned to Germany to an interrogation camp there. He stayed in the States for a number of years, helping the Americans with their propaganda war over the issue of Korea. The Central Intelligence Agency knew he was a vital asset for this work, as their knowledge of his background and his published articles proved just how good he was at his job. According to the Americans, he was one of the earliest pioneers of brainwashing and had successfully carried this out on American and Allied prisoners of war and brought them round to his way of thinking. He was very persuasive without being obvious about it. It is important to note that men with the same strong attributes as d'Alquen were already being employed in the CIA, but what he gave was more profound as he had changed an entire nation's outlook for over ten years. It was during this time that his first marriage fell apart.

During his time in captivity, relations were strained between him and Erika. She had not shared his ideology and their years apart meant a split was almost inevitable. They had written to each other in 1947, but slowly the letters dried up and in 1953, Gunter and Erica divorced, going their separate ways.

D'Alquen returned to Germany after his spell in the United States, remarried and had two more children, Ingo and Diana, with his second wife, Angela Kranz. He was employed as a textile manufacturer. His greatest regret was that he was never allowed to publish works again. It had been his career for so long and now he was forbidden from doing what he loved. In July 1955, at a de-nazification court in Berlin, he was fined 60,000 DM because of his role in Hitler's Germany. Three years later he was hit by another fine of 28,000 DM, having been found guilty of incitement to murder by means of publication. The court believed he had wallowed in anti-Semitism and glorified the SS and all that they stood for and, worst of all, he had been paid for it.

D'Alquen died in 1998, but throughout his life he denied ever knowing about any genocide plans, even though his newspaper, and others, had printed material confirming that concentration camps were up and running in Germany and Poland.

Gunter d'Alquen had been labelled a 'black' Nazi, or 'C+' by the screening process and, as such, was sent to the most secure prisoner of war camp in the United Kingdom. He was again screened at Watten but his status did not change. His writings and role in the Third Reich had made him dangerous as far as the British were concerned, yet his skills proved incredibly useful to the propaganda machine of the Central Intelligence Agency in the United States in the run up to the Korean War in the 1950s. His time at Watten was merely a few months but he allowed the camp to have a written record by way of the publication of the monthly magazine *Der Wattener* and gave the men some kind of record from their own point of view on captivity and news from the letters they received from home. It is rumoured that there is still a copy of this in Caithness. Perhaps there are others abroad. But whatever else, Gunter d'Alquen had a profound effect on Nazi Germany, post-war Britain and the United States of America in its war on Communism.

Chapter 7

Local Memories

————————

Many local people remember the camp at Watten, but only a few are willing to speak of it. During the time it was in the village, the local residents had been told, like Herr Schoon, not ever to speak or write of the camp. Photographs were forbidden. Yet, today, sixty years later, the cloud of secrecy is beginning to dissipate and gives an interesting insight on how the camp was viewed from the outside.

During the summer of 2005, local man Robert Miller spoke of how the area where the camp was built was known years afterwards, and long after it had all but disappeared, as 'The Camps'. This took in Achingale Place, the top path along the football field and park, down Bain Place and back along the main road. He also spoke of how one young German soldier had a somewhat mischievous streak.

The prisoners used to march round the village, but one of them never managed the walk. He would stop off at a local house where he had a bowl of porridge then he would join the line of soldiers as they returned to the camp. However, this was fairly uncommon. The soldiers knew that if they were caught where they were not supposed to be, they would be punished. But perhaps what would have been worse was that the local police might have charged the family who had been providing the food. Still, it was obviously worth the risk. Rations at the camp were adequate but there was no way any of the soldiers would have refused some extra food, especially during the winter months.

Mr and Mrs McCarthy of the village recall their memories of the camp. Mr McCarthy is a native of Caithness although his wife comes from the south of Scotland and over the years he has told her of the various things that happened with men at the camp.

> We built our house in 1973 on the ground that was used as part of the hospital complex. The Nissen huts were demolished in the 1960s but they left the rusty barbed wire. There was a great big Nissen hut opposite us, which was their concert hall and theatre and there was a big bit at the back for the cinema screen. Latterly it was used as an agricultural store before the new house was built on its site. When we had moved in we started to think

about our garden. As we worked, we found concrete paths and the concrete foundation of a Nissen hut. We found numerous pill bottles, broken crockery and smashed glass. For years we dug up barbed wire. We never found any bones! We found out later, when a former prisoner returned to Watten, that the foundation that we had discovered was where the dentist worked when the camp was functioning. He asked if he could have a look around and pointed, saying 'Ah, dentist hut'. That was the first we knew about it. Also, the rhubarb and raspberry canes that go up the road too must have been put there by the prisoners.

These raspberry canes line the road from Watten to Mybster for a good few hundred yards. They still bear fruit to this day. The prisoners must have been allowed to plant them out in the spring and pick the fruit when it was ready in the autumn. Slightly behind the canes is evidence of the barbed wire that surrounded the camp.

Mr McCarthy remembers a soldier escorting a prisoner around the village, who always had a book with him. Every time he saw him, he was reading. He was an older man, and was 'more professional looking'. This soldier was often seen by other members of the public, with his book in his hand, which is what made him stand out from the others. He also remembers the goat the family had when he was young.

We had a white goat when we lived down the Strath Road, and it used to be tethered to the side of the road. I remember German soldiers there, nursing it. They must have been of country stock because they knew about goats.

Mrs McCarthy puts the point forward that: 'You can imagine being incarcerated in a prison maybe in a war that you didn't really want to take part in and something like that would be uplifting'. This is very true. Many soldiers took great delight in these moments of normality. Something as simple as this could lift their spirits and take them back to a memory of life before the war back home in Germany. Yet, on the other hand, it may have been the case that the soldiers were hungry and while they knew about goats, maybe took the opportunity to help themselves to some milk because they were hungry.

Mr McCarthy speaks of the very special delivery of a letter after the war that he found incredible.

We were working on a house at Milton, a few miles from Wick and the people on the croft were speaking to us. They told us about a letter. Now the road to the house goes up to the top of a hill and at that time it was a working croft. The couple that had the croft must have had a German working for them in late 1947 or early 1948. They told us that he had written that he couldn't remember their address and hoped the letter would get to them. On the envelope he had written their name, with the address as 'The House on the Hill, Outside Wick'. That was the address. But the postman delivered it to them.

This was not unusual. Many prisoners when they returned home wanted to keep in touch with some of the local families because they had worked for them and had found kindness. They had been embraced into family life with no questions asked. However, addresses would get lost when the soldiers were returning home and many wanted to keep in touch. Therefore by using their initiative and writing the rough directions of where they worked, as well as the family's name, letters often were delivered. This was also because at that time, the local postmen were able to deliver letters that were wrongly, or sketchily, addressed to the person they were addressed to. Today in Scotland, letters are delivered to the address rather than the person they are addressed to so if these kinds of letters were sent today, it is possible they would never have been delivered and all contact would have been lost.

The McCarthy's describe what they remember of the layout of the camp.

> When the council took over the land where the camp was, they never bothered changing the roads. The roads are the originals. There were huts on both sides of the roads and they went up to Bain Place. Opposite Flett's Garage on the main road in the village was the dump for the camp. Originally it was low lying land and they filled it with bottles and tins. When the new house was built there, they had a job putting in the foundations because of the dump.

All of the waste went into this dump, although not food or human waste. Tin, bottles and packets were taken over and deposited. By the time the camp closed, the rubbish was piled above the pit, so it had to be crushed down then filled in. A few years later there was no evidence of the dump whatsoever as the grass covered it and this looked as if it had been there for years. Remarkably, no one remembers a smell coming from the dump. However they do remember another smell.

One day in particular stands out in the memories of the local population – the day the bung dropped out. Mr and Mrs McCarthy take up the story.

> The water supply for the camp came from the loch and the sewage went back down to the loch. But that was just for the main part of the camp. The rest was what you would call dry. The sewage was carted away from the prisoners' camp in a square tank on a little lorry and it had to come down to the main road a wee bit and then up towards the back of the camp to be spread on the fields. One day, the bung that was in the tank came out in the village. It left a trail and the smell was terrible.

Sandy Sutherland as a young boy also remembers the incident.

> The camp had no drainage for the sewerage and I remember it being taken from the camp by a tanker and spread on the fields opposite Banks Lodge. The day the bung fell out, everyone will remember. The smell was awful, and you could see the trail all over the road.

The tanker arrived several times a week to gather the waste. Its route never changed, taking the wet sewage from the camp, travelling down onto the main road then turning up towards the fields at the back of the camp. It was recycling in a fairly primitive way, but it was good for the soil. A company near Stirling does much the same today. However, when the bung fell out, some of the raw waste ended up on the roads, creating a smell the village had never experienced before. It did not help that the weather was warm at the time. From that day onwards, the bung was thoroughly checked, not only to make sure there was no repeat of the incident, but also to make sure the farmers got their 'manure'.

Mr Sutherland remembers the men marching and singing German songs as he watched as a child. He also describes the camp.

> There was a detention centre just behind 4 and 5 Achingale Place and I've been in there. There were swastikas on the wall with rude messages such as 'English Pigs' and worse. But some of the men were fine. We used to go to the parties in the camp with music. They called themselves an orchestra but it was more like a travelling band, like a big band. And we used to get toys that they made.

The toy which Sandy cherishes is a puzzle made from twisted metal. The two pieces are looped together but if done correctly, they will separate. One part looks like a love heart while the other is a rounded triangle with a large pin going through two loops at the base of it. The prisoners also made a wooden cart that he and his sister played with and many happy times were had in it. In addition to the puzzle, Mr Sutherland has in his possession a beautifully carved rectangular wooden box, which was also a product of the camp. Handmade, it is in excellent condition and, unlike many others who put these kind of things away in a cupboard to gather dust, Mr Sutherland uses the box which is on display. The lid has been carved so that it looks like four gentle triangles meeting at a flat square top on which is a diagonally-placed square handle.

Among other items made by the men were wooden submarines carved from any wood the men found lying around. Sacks were made into slippers and they also made beautiful cigarette holders, which they sold to the locals. These kinds of crafts kept the men occupied and gave the children of the county especially an everlasting image of the men who made them toys.

Sandy Sutherland and his sister were given the play cart by the prisoners who made it.

The Sutherland family also inherited a dog from the inner compound when the camp closed. A British soldier named Alfie had left the dog and the Sutherland family had the animal for many years.

Mr Sutherland remembers the prisoners' clothing and a prisoner who visited the family.

> The prisoners had a diamond on their back and we used to say it was a target for if they escaped. But I don't know if that was the reason. It would distinguish them from everyone else. Otto Hager used to come to my folks' house, which was down by the railway. There was another camp at the station but it wasn't a prisoner of war camp. He was trusted. He came back to see us in the 1970s, but he was too late to see Mum and Dad. He saw my sister but didn't stay too long because it was too cold.

Again this is something backed up by many people. The prisoners found the Scottish weather inclement. Although Germany does suffer from cold weather and deep snows in the winter, it was not so cold as it was in Caithness. Because of where the county lies, the summers were not generally all that warm and the winters were freezing. It did not help that it was also a very windy area. Gales and severe gales are commonplace, but it is something that local people are used to, so they found it strange that the prisoners made such a fuss over the weather. As mentioned, in the Red Cross reports, an extra blanket was issued to each prisoner because of the inclement conditions.

Mr Sutherland goes on to speak of the football matches.

> I used to go and watch them play. I remember them playing the Thurso Swifts but no other team. It was good. They played in the field with the standing stone by the river and they marched down, singing.

The field in question lies next to the Wick River, just on the left hand side of the road that goes into the county town of Wick, just over the Achingale Bridge. It is low lying and between autumn and spring, the field sometimes floods. However, because it is so flat, it was the ideal place to have football matches. There was a football field at the camp, but because of security, the Swifts had to play the men at this field. Many of the villagers, as well as those from the surrounding area, watched these matches when they were on and the crowds were delighted by the thrill of the game.

In the winter, Mr Sutherland recalls the mischief-makers from the British side. 'The soldiers at the camp used to throw snowballs at us at the school. I remember that. That was the soldiers though, not the prisoners.' It is unclear whether the prisoners were discouraged from doing this or simply just did not think on doing it, but the British guards took great delight in the pastime. The children would scurry past on their way to the school and suddenly be hit on the backs by giant snowballs. Some of the children retaliated. Many did not for fear of the soldier coming out and giving them what for. Luckily for the soldiers, this new game never got back to Lt.-Col. Murray.

Margaret Thurso, widow of the late Robin Macdonald Sinclair, 2nd Viscount Thurso, remembers the camp well. In a letter she writes: 'As far as I know, the camp was received if not enthusiastically, at least with equanimity in the village. To begin with, a Polish guard of soldiers looked after the security of the camp and they mingled freely with the local people.'

She remembers that the local Polish captain dined with her family at the Old Manse in North Watten on many occasions. She also remembers that Lt.-Col Murray and Captain Tim Gunn, who was himself a prisoner of war in Germany for a time, were in charge of the camp.

One memory stands out for her from her visits to the camp.

> I vividly remember being invited to the camp one Christmas and it was perfectly beautiful. The Germans, who celebrated Christmas in a big way, unlike Caithnessians who tended to celebrate New Year in those days, produced a real fir tree and decorated it with real, pure white candles. It was simple and very beautiful, and I have never forgotten it.

Again, this enthusiasm for Christmas was in an ICRC report. Being young at the time, it must have been magical to the children to see a fir tree decorated with candles. This was in the camp itself and the men had saved up for the candles. Of course, they also received candles from the Red Cross and these too were placed on the tree. The guards were impressed by the decorations as well and this cheered them up while they were away from their own families for Christmas.

Another local remembers how, as a young girl in the Wick Guides, they were taken to a concert. Margaret Shearer explains what it was like.

> As a special treat for doing well in tests, Captain Wallace and Lieutenant Sutherland would take us along to the monthly musical concert held behind the barbed wire in the Nissen huts at Watten. It was a wonderful experience to be able to sit back in very uncomfortable cold seats, and often rain – another noisy accompaniment. We were told by the conductor to sit back, relax and close our eyes. Here we were, schoolgirls enjoying some wonderful music far from the comfort of the music halls but equally delightful as these talented musicians entertained us. Hatred gone out the windows and love in no small measure came through the barbed wire of that encampment. All is forgiven as we listened to Beethoven.

She goes on to explain that only four to six Guides would gain entrance at a time, and that it was a treat 'to hear such a feast of music'. In the opening paragraph of her letter, she writes: 'I wonder if anyone else has such fond memories of the POW Camp at Watten as I have'. The camp was obviously well liked.

These gifted musicians had the greatest effect on Caithness and it is the musical evenings that most people remember with a great deal of fondness. In the main, the music was classical and included the works of Mozart, Beethoven and Schubert. The music would fill the air surrounding the camp so even if people were unable to gain access to the camp theatre, they could still hear it being played. Special concerts were put on at Christmas but every week music was played. The prisoners could lose themselves in their music and remove themselves from being prisoners to being performers, much to the delight of the audiences they drew in.

Hector Sutherland made a friend with one of the prisoners as they were thrown together on a farm, working the harvest.

> I worked at Knockglass Farm at Spittal in 1946. The prisoner had come to work on the farm and we were both sent out to 'stook' the sheaves. What a lovely boy he was, fair hair, blue eyes and he told me his age. He was eight-

*Fritz Ziegelbauer, a young prisoner at the
camp, was an SS man and had been a guard
at Berchtesgaden, Hitler's summer retreat.*

een, two years younger than me. He was called Fritz Ziegelbauer. He knew
no English and I knew no German. We worked away together and soon we
were beginning to understand one another. He had a wrist watch. I had none,
so we started with the time in German and English. Gradually I learned the
German time, and him the English. He stayed with us for six months, going
back to Watten every night, and by that time I had learned a lot of the
language. I was sorry when he left, for he told me many stories of Germany,
Russia and France, having been captured at Caen in 1944. He wrote after he
left, but he said, 'I never come again to Scottland'. He was an SS man, who
had been in the Hitler Youth, and had seen Hitler a few times.

Mr Sutherland remembers the young soldier telling him that he had also been a guard
at Berchtesgaden, Hitler's summer retreat in the mountains. Berchtesgaden lies in the German
Bavarian Alps near the border with Austria, some thirty kilometres or so from Salzburg and
it was here that Adolf Hitler had his mountain residence, Berghof. Berghof was a sumptuous
home, bought by the money he had made from his book *Mein Kampf.* Among the many people
to visit or work at Berghof were Max Wünsche, Hitler's one-time personal aid and a prisoner
at Watten, Martin Bormann, head of the Party Chancellory and Hitler's private secretary, and
his wife, Albert Speer, his chief architect and Minister for Armaments and his wife, Josef 'Sepp'
Dietrich, one of the closest men to Hitler and commander of 6 SS-Panzerkorps, and Frtiz Witt,
who commanded the 12 SS-Panzer-Divison Hitler-Jugend before his death in Normandy in
1944. Others included the Goebbels family, all of whom perished in Hitler's Bunker in Berlin
in 1945. Many of these visitors were served their meals, made by Hitler's personal chef Herr

Kannenberg, and drinks on the terrace under the shade of the canvas umbrellas with the spectacular view over to his native Austria as a backdrop.

Berghof was palatial. The original Haus Wachenfeld had been built in 1916 and was rather modest in size. In the later 1920s Hitler rented the house and fell in love with it, so secured the right to purchase it if it was ever to be sold. Hitler bought it for the grand some of 40,000 Goldmarks in 1933 and commissioned architect Alois Degano to remodel the house fit for the Führer. It was greatly extended and incorporated into Berghof, including its terrace, which looked over the mountains, giving spectacular views. The grand staircase from the driveway at the house was used as a backdrop for many photographs including ones of his more elite visitors such as the Duke and Duchess of Windsor. The inside of the house was lavishly decorated although all the rooms were painted green. Persian carpets adorned the floors, tapestries ornamented the walls and original paintings hung in every room. Hitler's office was large and richly furnished with his conference room much in the same décor. The living areas were just as richly decked out, with chandeliers, exquisite soft furnishings and again Persian rugs. Fresh flowers were picked every day and placed in many of the rooms including the Great Room, the dining-room and sunroom. Even the small private sitting-rooms and bedrooms of Hitler and his mistress Eva Braun received the same delicate attention. The guest bedrooms had engravings on the walls and some of Hitler's own art was on display. His library at the house was filled with books on architecture, painting and history, a passion for which he had throughout his life. On the western side of Berghof was the Adjutancy building where Max Wünsche, his one-time aid, must have stayed. The house even had a landing strip, for he owned his own private aeroplane and it made it easier for his generals and friends to visit him.

Every day Hitler would take a walk at nine o'clock with his gardeners. The gardens at Berghof boasted not only shrubs and roses, but also a well-stocked kitchen garden. He was a life-long vegetarian and his chef came up with many different dishes for him to try, using vegetables only from the garden. When guests came for dinner, he did provide them with meat, chicken or fish, such as venison, duck and salmon, and this would be served with the finest wines he had in his cellar. Yet Hitler himself never drank or smoked. Hitler's last visit to his beloved Berghof was in July 1944.

In May 1945 American troops of the 3rd Infantry Division captured Berghof, a week or so after it had suffered damage from direct hits from a bombing raid by the RAF. SS troops had set the house alight by the time the Americans had arrived and later that day they took down the swastika. The house smouldered for days. In the 1950s the Bavarian Government decided it would be wise to destroy the house completely as much of its shell was still in tact and they believed it would be a Mecca for neo-Nazis. In 1952 the house disappeared, although the garage remained. It was dismantled three years later. Today, on the anniversary of Hitler's birthday, 20 April, some German war veterans and neo-Nazis leave flowers and light candles in memory of Hitler and his life at Berchtesgaden.

Although all these memories so far are by local people, one other source is vitally important to understand what life was like for the prisoners from someone else's perspective. In 1946, *The Scotsman* newspaper sent a reporter to Caithness to investigate. The following article appeared on 16 September and can be found at www.archive.scotsman.com.

Excerpt from: **The Scotsman** – 16th September 1946

GERMAN P.o.W. IN CAITHNESS

Harvesting Work
and Surveying

IT WAS SURPRISING TO STEP into Wick and see a group of Germans making a survey of the town. It was even more surprising to notice a German and a Scots Guardsman walking side by side along Bridge Street – one of the principle thoroughfares – and attracting but slight attention, and that, apparently, from visitors.

I knew that there was a P.o.W. camp at Watten, beside the loch of that name, in the heart of Caithness, but I was not prepared to find these transient residents occupying so large a place in the life of the community. This is the main reason.

Agriculture is by far the most important industry in the county. There is a chronic – and apparently increasing – scarcity of farm-workers; and production is far above peace-time levels. Up to and including 1943, soldiers helped to ingather the grain. Few of these were available in 1944 – another harvest of unhappy memory. Now, for the second year, Germans are filling the gap.

My first encounter with these men was when a dozen of them arrived at a farm where I was a guest, to single turnips. They were in their thirties and forties, and the average height must have been six feet. With hoes at the slope they marched, though not in formation, in the manner which popular belief ascribes to Prussian Guards. They were escorted by a diminutive Irishman with a rifle. That was in June 1945. Now the formality of guarding those who go outside the camp has been abandoned. Escape to Germany is practically impossible. From time to time a few make a break from the camp, but they are quickly captured, usually on the road to the south.

The routine is for the men to arrive by lorry at their place of work each morning; in the evening groups of them await the return of the lorries at convenient assembly points. Some are billeted on farms.

The Germans at Watten [Vötten to them] are divided into two categories. The obdu-

Excerpt from: **The Scotsman** – 16th September 1946

rate Nazis remain behind barbed wire. It is the others, those who are prepared to make the best of a bad job, who go out to work on parole. These men are hard working, competent, and careful. Few have had agricultural experience but they are willing to learn, and they can be trusted to do whatever task is assigned to them. The Wick survey is an example. A group of whom I talked contained only one surveyor. The others were learning as they worked. The chief of the survey is said to be a former assistant to Dr Todt. Their map will facilitate house-building and town-planning.

The Germans go about their work unobtrusively. They are ready to respond to a salute or a smile, and are grateful for any little act of courtesy or kindness. Their bearing, allied to industry and capacity, has won them a considerable measure of respect. The farmers frankly like them. The men now in the county appear to be in their twenties and thirties. They have much less of the parade ground manner than their comrades who were there last year.

The Watten concerts are now so well established a feature of Caithness life that a guide book includes them among the attrac-

tions of the county! They are held each Wednesday evening, and a bus is run from Wick for the convenience of patrons. It is chartered by the 'military authorities', and a lance-corporal who took the fares informed me that the proceeds go to some British soldiers' fund.

It was on a wet and stormy night that I went to Watten, and more than forty of us had to endure the discomforts of travelling in a vehicle seated for twenty. We were 'decanted' into a Nissen hut, seated for about 200, which was well filled. The band consisted of half a dozen violins, a violincello, a double bass, a piano, and a few wind instruments. The stage on to which the players, to the number of 16 or 17, crowded, was so small that elbow room must have presented difficulty.

When the curtain was drawn aside a stern-faced conductor, in battle-dress blouse dyed green and service trousers, stepped a short pace forwards to the edge of the platform and made a formal bow. There was a mild clapping of hands. The opening piece, March of the Fliers by Dostal, was heartily applauded. Schubert, Mozart, and Wagner followed, and the penultimate item was Blue Bonnets over the

Excerpt from: **The Scotsman** – 16th September 1946

Border. The audience was most appreciative, indeed, enthusiastic. The writer, who makes no pretence to knowledge of music, must content himself saying that never before had he heard such a concert.

Not a word was spoken during the performance. Everything was correct, even to the playing of God Save the King.

While the instruments spoke with effect, the players remained impassive. They watched their music and the conductor, and I did not see one of them glance at the audience until the close. Once or twice, the conductor relaxed into a grave smile. The only expression was the tenor who sang, with great animation, two songs in German.

What of the attitude of the local people? Perhaps the best indication is given by the action of a farm worker who had lost a leg in the war. After dinner he offered a cigarette to the German billetee at the other side of the kitchen table. 'Why shouldn't I?' he asked when someone expressed surprise. 'I don't expect he wanted the war any more than I did.' The farmer's wife, herself hard pressed by many duties, was seeking a German grammar course to brush up on her slight knowledge of the language, and enable her to alleviate the loneliness of a man who had no English, by speaking a few words to him in his own tongue. At another farm an obliging lad – he a little more than out of his 'teens – is regarded with affection by a family, two members of which fell in the war of 1914–18.

Another view was expressed by a crofter who wrathfully demanded to know why Germans were working in Caithness when they were greatly needed at home, and 'our own people are on the dole'.

The opinion is widely held that, the war being over, the men should be allowed to go home. Farmers, with their own difficulties in mind, may not always subscribe to it, but they feel strongly that a much higher proportion of their wages should be paid to the men, who receive only a pittance.

There may be, doubtless is, some animosity, but I did not come across it. Not the least remarkable aspect of the situation is the speed with which the emotional wounds of war appear to be healing.

The Scotsman article begins with the men doing their survey of the town. This is an important element in the history of the camp. A local Watten woman, Cathy Macadie, had lived in Watten as a young girl and remembered that some of the German prisoners were architects and draughtsmen. They had been allowed to work in the Caithness County Council offices in Wick with Mr James Henderson, who was in charge of the architects department and designed local authority housing in Caithness.

James Murie Henderson was born before the outbreak of the First World War and studied at the Glasgow School of architecture. He joined the Royal Burgh Office of Rutherglen in 1938 but was called up and saw military action, serving as a pilot before being injured and discharged in 1942. Within weeks he had been appointed chief architect to Rolls Royce Ltd at their Glasgow factory. When he finished at Rolls Royce, he was recalled to Rutherglen before being given the opportunity to serve as County Architect and Planning Officer for Caithness County Council in 1944. He was wholly responsible for the office and it was here that he made his biggest impact on the county by engaging Caithness stone and slate into buildings, both on their exteriors and interiors and in the fire places. Henderson designed the houses in the square named after him in the village following in the footsteps of Sir Basil Spence, who designed Thurso High School and Coventry Cathedral, and who had designed houses in Dunbar, East Lothian, where they have deep recessed arched entrances built by using Caithness stone and slates, much in the same design as Henderson Square. Henderson's designs can also be seen in Castletown and in some areas of Wick. He was to leave the Council in 1946 for an appointment had come up in Trinidad. However, after being there only a short time, in 1950 he died as a result of an accident, aged 37.

An illustration exists of parts of Watten that was drawn by the men of Camp 165 and in Wick Mrs Mary Thompson has framed on her wall the design for her house, drawn up by the Surveying Team Camp 165, which is dated 5 November 1947. The plan also shows the adjoining properties and their gardens, but Mrs Thompson's house has the inscription below stating, 'Harrowfield, Hause of Mr James Robertson'. The spelling of 'Hause' is important, as it is a combination of English and German. She found the plans rolled up in a cupboard when she moved into the property.

Dr Todt, as mentioned in *The Scotsman* article, was an engineer and founder of Organisation Todt. After World War I, Fritz Todt joined a civil engineering company having studied advanced engineering at Karlsruhe, and by 1938 had founded the Organisation, which was responsible for the construction of the Seigfried Line. In 1940 he was appointed Reichsminister für Bewaffnung und Munition, the Reich minister for Armaments and Munitions. In 1942, when he was leaving the Wolf's Lair at Ratenburg after a meeting with Hitler, his plane exploded and he was killed. He was succeeded as Reichsminister by Albert Speer.

In an anonymous e-mail, a writer recalls his memories of the camp. He remembered there were a few escape attempts and recalls one prisoner being returned to the camp 'the following morning and asked to be taken in again as there was nowhere for him to run to'. He goes on to mention the concerts and how 'a bus load of us went with our mothers and there we saw a really good show'. During their internment, the prisoners of war 'went round the doors selling rope shoes and bags which they had made – many of us wore the shoes. I can remember them goose-stepping towards the brae where they were building, or dismantling air raid shelters'.

The Red Hackle magazine of the Black Watch shows yet another side to the camp. According to an article published in the January issue of 1963, Watten was classed as having 'all the hardest cases, submarine crews, etc'. Yet one young man, Neil Ritchie, came back from a visit to the camp in the 1940s, enthusing to the writer of the article, who is anonymous, that he 'must go up and see Tishy at Watten. He has a first-class show and incidentally gave me a better lunch than I have had since war broke out'. The author of the article eventually did this and remembers his coat being taken by a 'most efficient German attendant', who was in fact Lt.-Col. Murray's butler. During the 'most sumptuous lunch', the orchestra had played for them and then afterwards they had sat down and watched a play especially put on by the prisoners for their visitor. He remembers little of the play itself, apart from one scene. This was set in a Bavarian inn and a guest was complaining to the innkeeper about all the flies in the lavatories. The innkeeper's retort was that the guest 'use the lavatory before breakfast when all the flies are in the kitchen'.

As for soldiers being billeted up to Watten, they were surprised by the length of time it took to arrive. In an article on the Caithness.org website, Frank Williams spoke to his niece about his experiences at Watten. He had been posted to Caithness in 1947, having spent time in India, so it must have been quite a shock in the climatic stakes. According to him the posting tended to work in alphabetical order so by the time he was chosen, he was sent up to the far north of Scotland. Like so many to arrive, he was struck by the remoteness of the county. He had travelled up from Norfolk and it had taken over twenty-six hours to reach Watten, a place he had never heard of. On arrival, Lt.-Col. Murray spoke to the men and advised them of the lack of entertainment in the area and that they would have to make their own entertainment. So this they did. Burns Night, a birthday, or any kind of anniversary, was celebrated. On Burns Night the men had haggis in the sergeants' mess with music provided by the prisoners. Under the charge of Sergeant Boxall, the prisoners cooked the haggis but because there was so much left over, it lasted for days being dressed up as rissoles, used in soup and put in sandwiches.

Mr Williams also said that when he arrived the Nissen huts were beginning to fall apart and the camp was fairly run-down. The corrugated sheets were no longer waterproof and rain dripped into the huts. Peat, dug by the prisoners, had now become the source of heat in the stoves. One of the other complaints by the prisoners was the food, especially the kippers. In Scotland, the heads are left on when they are served and this did not go down well with the Germans.

During their time as prisoners, some were taken down to the LDC for interrogation as mentioned earlier. Mr Williams accompanied some of these men down on the train, alighting at Euston station almost thirty-six hours later. His gripe was the food the prisoners had to take with them. As a serving soldier, Mr Williams had the usual sandwiches and cake whereas the Germans, much to his annoyance, opened up their packed lunch boxes to a boiled egg, cheeses and ham. He reckoned they got the food from the local farmers as part payment for all their hard work.

Mr Williams married a local girl, one of many men who were to do so. He had just celebrated his twenty-first birthday at the camp.

After the German prisoners had been repatriated many wrote back to the families they had worked with. One striking letter was written by Hans Sepp, kindly reproduced here, including spelling errors, by permission of Mrs Rosie in Thurso. It is dated 18.7.51:

> *Dear Jimmy, dear Mrs Bridge, dear Alec,*
>
> *Maybe you thought Hans has forgotten you. Not at all! I was very often with my head and my thoughts with you. When I arrived here at the place where I got the job, I had to bring in order many things so that I had to be very busy. I also had to start work at once. It does mean I was very busy. Now I am settled down all-right and I got more time for writing and so on. Please don't be angry that I didn't write earlier. I hope we remain the friends we always had been. That I returned to Germany that will make no difference to our friendship anyway but it does mean we are a little further apart geographically speaking though in no other way. If only nations could be as friendly as individuals the world would be a very nice place to live in. This may came, but not I am afraid, in our time.*
>
> *I got in my job very well. Certainly I miss my open-air life but I shall get used to my new office-job in time too. The life here is quite a different one compared with the life in Caithness because the town life provides many occasions to enjoy. On the other side the climate in Caithness is much healthier than it is here. The mid-summer is very hot here and I can't stand a terrible heat.*
>
> *Things are not yet very good in Germany as everything is very expensive. We don't need a ration-book and all the shops are filled with goods of every kind but people have no money. I am quite well off myself so that I can help and look after my parents too and that satisfies me. I have got a good job and I like it. I have got a lovely furnished room ... Sometimes I take a walk in a nice place, sometimes I make a trip to the town Frankfurt to see a great football match or to pay a visit to the opera. You see I don't feel lonely ...*
>
> *Please remember me to ... John Allan, Mrs Bruce, Mr Sutherland (Tacher), Mrs Sutherland (Mary), young Hector and – I nearly forgot, isn't it awful – Mary McGregor.*
>
> *Very best wishes,*
>
> *Yours,*
> *Hans*

This letter demonstrates just how close the prisoners felt to the local families they worked for and the feeling was reciprocated. Mrs Rosie believes this was the last the family ever heard from Hans 'Sepp'. Sepp's last known whereabouts was Groß-Umsadt, Hesse, Germany.

In another letter by a man simply known as 'Gerhard' he too speaks of his return to Germany and sends his best wishes to the family. He felt lucky that he had returned home but remembered working at the water-pump station at the camp. He was later transferred to Camp 63 in Perthshire and it was here that he got the news he was waiting for. On Christmas Eve he was told he was to be freed and return home. He gained his release on 16 January 1948. He was demobbed in the American Zone and stayed with an aunt before going to his sister who was by now in the Russian Zone. He was one of the lucky ones when he got back to Germany as he got a job as a motor mechanic. As for food though, he could only take a small piece of bread with him and was constantly hungry. Whilst in captivity at Watten, he sometimes received some milk and butter from a local family and 'I will say my best thanks for all wath you have done for us', he wrote to them. He ended the letter 'I send you my best greetings and best wishes for your hohl live time … from a German boy. Gerhard'.

Both of these letters demonstrate the kind of relationships within Caithness between the prisoners and the civilian population. It was one of mutual respect and genuine friendship. Unlike Herr Schoon in Chapter 3 who has a lifelong relationship with the Caithness family he worked for, these two men sadly lost touch with the families they had befriended. It is unknown what happened to them.

Margaret Hammerton and Kathleen Hooker's father, Lance Corporal Jack Hooker, served as a guard at Camp 165.

Jack Hooker had been born in West Croydon near London in 1925 and served in the Royal Artillery. The regiment was sent to Durban then transferred by troop-ship to Bombay. En route, they saw the stricken HMS *Ramalees*, which had a hole through its midships although it was somehow still managing to stay afloat. While at Trincomalee in Ceylon (Sri Lanka), Mr Hooker suffered a burst ear drum due to the Japanese bombing the local harbour. Despite this injury which left him deaf in one ear, he was transferred to the 1st Battalion Royal Warwickshires where he saw action in Rangoon, Mandalay and finally Singapore. In August 1945 the Japanese were hit by the atomic weapons which ended the war in the east. This came as a great surprise to the troops who had expected the war to drag on.

From the Far East Mr Hooker was transferred and began his tour of duty at Watten in January 1946. Unbeknown to him, he was guarding Ludwig Schoon. Many years later the two men met at Gatwick Airport in August 1998 as they headed for Caithness, and they began talking, revealing that both had been at Camp 165, although they had never met in the 1940s. Since the chance meeting, the two men remained firm friends. According to Mr Hooker in an interview with a local newspaper, 'It was quite a coincidence', although it is no surprise the two men never met due to the numbers of captives.

During his time at the camp, Mr Hooker met Betty Steven, a local girl, who worked in the post office. This was owned by her sister and brother-in-law, Kathleen and Mowat McAddie. The McAddies owned a café as well in which the young Betty also worked and it was in the café in Station Road in Watten that Jack met his future wife. Whilst courting, the couple enjoyed their walks around Loch Watten when time, and weather, allowed. On 25 October 1946, the young couple married in Watten Church and had their reception in Watten Hall then settled at Puldagon near Stirkoke by Wick.

When Mr Hooker was released from the army, he had an exemplary record. According to Captain Gunn who filled in the Notification of Impending Release form, he was 'a smart and clean NCO. He is entirely trustworthy'. He acted as caterer in the sergeants' mess for the period of a year. The date of his release from Watten to the Royal Army Reserve was 19 October 1946. He was awarded the 1939–45 Star, the Burma Star and the Defence Medal.

Mr Hooker met up with Herr Schoon on several occasions but sadly Mr Hooker died in 2007.

Captain Gunn's time at Watten can be compared to Lt.-Col. Murray's. He, like Murray, had been a prisoner of war and with this insight, used this knowledge at Watten to make sure the prisoners were treated much better than he had been. Tim Gunn had been a student at Edinburgh Academy where he gained a Certificate A which automatically meant a commission, but he had already joined up and had gone up to Oxford for one and a half years, but left through illness. His father had been a colonel in the Camerons and was keen for his son to join up. He joined the 1st Battalion Cameron Highlanders in 1938 and stayed at Catterick Camp under Col. Wembley, who was later to become General Wembley, the commander of the 51st Division. When war broke out, he was at home at Inverness at the Cameron barracks. He got annoyed at Captain William Mackay who was able to sit back while the men were 'going to be slaughtered'. He went down to Aldershot and shortly after that, was sent to France, firstly to Cherbourg when he went with the transport. He went from Cherbourg to the Belgian frontier to a place called Orczy. This was to the north-west of the Maginot Line. The first thing the men had to do was to build trenches, but there was the problem of very few trees. With no trees for wood, trenches could not be built. There were four battalions in the brigade during this part of the Phoney War. The troops managed to acquire a wireless to hear the BBC news and keep up to date with what was happening. His colonel would come in and ask 'Are we at war today?' to which Gunn would reply, 'Not today sir'.

At that time, some of the men were wearing the kilt but the War Office wanted the men to get rid of it and put on battle-dress but the colonel fought this. As compensation for losing the kilt, the men were issued with the Blue Hackle.

Captain Gunn was sent back to Dieppe due to illness and on to England before being sent to the depot at Inverness, although the battalion was away, and only staff remained. He returned to France in the 4th Battalion Cameron Highlanders, who were based at Bayeux in the spring of 1940 when time passed slowly. From there the men went up to the Maginot Line, and onwards through the Line, being bombarded by German fire at the same time as the Germans had surrounded Dunkirk.

The men were then ordered go south of Paris to near the Somme to form a new line and journeyed by train to their positions. They reached the Somme and were heavily attacked. The men withdrew to the outskirts of St Valery, which was a sea of flames and when on the beach, Gunn saw a British ship being heavily shelled. The men marched along, both Germans and the British, and in the confusion were captured by the Germans. They were allowed to have some of their rations and marched through Belgium and Holland. Over 7000 men were captured at St Valery. The longest distance they ever walked was thirty miles in one day. They were not allowed breakfast and only when they arrived at their destination did they get anything to eat. A German soldier told Captain Gunn that it was going to be a very hard fight.

However, the men were shown a great deal of kindness by the local French people who left pails of milk on the roadside for the men to drink. He remembers crossing the frontier at Tourne and went into the local jail, which was bliss to them as they had been sleeping in the open, and Gunn got a cell all to himself. When the rations were being handed out, they got a barrel of herrings from Wick. The way the Germans treated the prisoners, however, was quite correct.

They had been marched through Belgium, on through Holland, onto a barge at Vaissel and travelled down the Rhine, being taken to a large Polish camp, run by Poles. These men were fellow prisoners of war. They were then transported to Bavaria and on to Laufen, an old German barracks near Salzburg, between Bavaria and Austria, right on the border. The first thing that they got were their heads shaved. The officers were segregated from the ordinary ranks at the Polish camp so Gunn was now in Offlag 7C. During his time there, a German quartermaster did not give the prisoners the rations they were supposed to get, which included potatoes and watery soup. Consequently, from being fourteen stones when he was captured, Captain Gunn's weight plummeted to nine.

The men made their own entertainment and were not allowed to work. This was an entirely British camp and the men formed an orchestra, the instruments being supplied by the Germans. They played *A Nightingale Sang in Berkley Square* and put on plays. The Church of Scotland sent parcels to the camp. When the men saw these, they were elated thinking they would contain all sorts of nice food, but when they opened them up the parcels contained Bibles and hymn books. The men were disappointed. As Captain Gunn puts it, 'It didn't matter if you died as long as you said your prayers'. The men had arrived in July 1940 and left in the spring of 1941.

From Laufen Captain Gunn was sent to Prosen in Poland. Surrounding Prosen there were eight forts with a moat around them. The countryside was flat. The men were transported by train and marched from the station, and all Gunn could see was a black hole and 'there standing … was a typical Prussian officer with a monocle in his eye and a peaked hat like a Kaiser hat … with a whip in his hand … but in actual fact he turned out a decent type'. Flees and lice were rife. This was another purely British camp, where Col. Todd was the senior British officer.

Captain Gunn remembers a successful escape attempt from the camp. Rubbish was taken over the drawbridge in a wooden container and one of the men escaped by placing rubbish on top of himself inside this box. 'We were in touch with the Polish underground and they got him out. We had an escape committee of course and anybody with any bright ideas would put it forward.'

At this camp the men got their proper rations. Red Cross parcels started to arrive at Prosen. 'The parcels most in demand were the Scottish ones', the captain recalls, 'because they had oatmeal in them and you could make porridge. There were cigarettes. I never smoked so I swapped them for Horlicks and Ovaltine. I think there were ten cigarettes, toilet paper, milk powder and sugar. Biscuits. I remember later on we got Canadian biscuits.'

The men got their battle rations too and the Germans never cut these when the Red Cross parcels came. As they were leaving Prosen, having been there for three or four months, they passed trainloads of troops heading to Russia for Operation Barbarossa. In the summer of 1941 the men were transported to another camp, which had been especially built for prisoners near Ulm. There was barbed wire round this camp and it was run by a man who the men nicknamed 'Death Warmed Up'. Here there were prisoners from Australia and New Zealand who had been captured in Crete. This camp held 1000 officers. An escape attempt was made by removing a steel stove from the middle of the room, and digging and tunnelling to the wire. The soil was distributed where the Germans rarely searched, but on this occasion they did and the attempt was aborted. Conditions were generally quite good inside the camp.

All of this helped Captain Gunn when he worked at Watten in that he knew what prisoner of war life had been like. He had experienced reduced rations and the need for news as well as the need for clothing, which put him in fine stead when commissioned with the task of working at Camp 165.

Chapter 8

Watten and the V2 Bomb

In 1947 Dr Paul Schröder was interrogated at the London District Cage for his part in the development of the V2 bomb at Peenemünde on the German Baltic coast near Poland. Under the tutelage of Dr Walter Dornberger, Schröder had been closely watched by the British and when captured, was sent to POW Camp 165, the most secure camp in the United Kingdom, because of his work.

In 1937 a huge rocket development site was established on the Baltic coast, where the missiles could be tested up to a range of two hundred miles. Originally, the test and development site was in Kummersdorf, an estate near Luckenwalde, some fifteen or so miles south of Berlin; however, it proved to be rather on the small side as war was fast approaching. Walter Dornberger and a group of researchers developed liquid-propelled rockets at the site in the early 1930s, which led to the development of the A1, A2, and A3 type rockets. It is thought that these rockets were initially for space flight as in the early 1930s war seemed unlikely, but they were prototypes with a much more deadly purpose. These A-type rockets were powered by ethanol and liquid oxygen. Ethanol was in good supply as Germany had refused to rely on crude oil because it was not always on hand. The Treaty of Versailles had forbidden the development of solid fuel rockets in Germany following World War I, but the Treaty had mentioned nothing about liquid fuel. This loophole paved the way for new, more dangerous kind of rocket, developed by Walter von Braun and Walter Dornberger during the 1930s. At Peenemünde the V1 and V2 began to take shape.

During numerous trials, the rockets had mixed fortunes initially, as the earlier ones needed redesigning, until the early 1940s. By 1941, the A5 rocket had been tested over seventy times. On 3 October 1942 the ultimate weapon had been created. On its test, it landed around one hundred and forty miles away and travelled at a height of about fifty miles, following its designated trajectory. The *Vergeltungswaffe 2* (Vengeance Weapon 2), or the V2 as it became better known, had been developed. The V2, a silent and incredibly aerodynamic ballistic missile, had a range of two hundred miles and carried a 2200 lb warhead. To propel the rocket took over 8000 lbs worth of fuel and it was guided by an internal navigational system, which controlled four external rudders on the tail fins and four internal ones near the motor. The fuel was pumped into the main chamber through over a thousand nozzles which in turn gave the correct mixture of alcohol and oxygen. Burning at around 2600°C, the water and ethanol mixture both cooled the chamber and heated the fuel. In order to ignite the fuel in the first place, two different types of self-igniting fuels were injected into the combustion chamber that created a spark and thus ignited the rocket. Gyroscopes were used to stabilise the rocket. Not designed to hit a specific target, the rocket would be able to inflict considerable damage on towns and cities in Europe.

What was so important about the V2 was the fact that it was silent. The V1, known as the Doodlebug, made a very distinctive noise, therefore giving a warning when it was coming. The engine was a simple jet engine, with a one-way air intake valve and combustion chamber which sounded like the buzzing noise of the Austrian insect that gave its name to the rocket when the shutters opened and closed due to the expanding gasses. Notorious for being directed at England and Belgium, the cities of London and Antwerp bore the brunt of these weapons when they were launched from sites all along the northern European coastline. Only with the introduction of a new radar system in the summer of 1944 did the V1 start being destroyed by automatic anti-aircraft guns as they entered British airspace. Attempts had been made with anti-aircraft batteries stationed along the English coast firing at the rockets to destroy them, and the RAF had tried shooting them down, but they proved too fast. However, Hawker Tempests were developed from Typhoons and could fly at low altitude and at speed. Between June and August 1944 over 600 V1s were shot down. Planes including Mosquitoes, Spitfires and Mustangs had all become involved in attempting to destroy them. The V2 on the other hand was immune to anti-aircraft fire quite simply because it dropped at almost four times the speed of sound.

Sites were sought in Occupied France from which to launch the rockets but this proved futile. Time and again these sites were targeted and destroyed by the British until Hitler finally conceded to mobile V2s. Around thirty trucks with massive trailers took the rocket to a site, including all the fuel it needed and men to construct it. It was put onto a launch table, fuelled, the gyroscopes placed in the appropriate section and armed. Then it was launched. This system was crucial to the Germans for the Allies failed to hit these mobile convoys and the rockets were launched from any chosen site, such as a forest or simply a roadside. In the end, sites included The Hague and the Hoek van Holland [Hook of Holland]. Mass production of the V2 began in earnest in late 1943 near Nordhausen in Thuringia in the heart of Germany, using Russian, French and Poles as slave labour. Hundreds of men died in the production of the rocket, mostly due to the cold and humidity but also the work itself was heavy and contributed to many deaths.

The first serious attack by V2s was launched against newly-freed Paris, followed by an attack on London. Antwerp and London received the full force of the V2 with over 90% of them targeted at these two cities. However, not all the rockets were successful. Hundreds blew up in mid-flight but that did not deter continued launchings. Over a matter of six months, more than three thousand hit their targets in England, Belgium, France, The Netherlands and even Germany itself. In England, Winston Churchill's government was able to play down the effects of the attacks as the Germans could not be sure their rockets had hit their targets or indeed landed. By keeping the news agencies in the dark over the true scale of the hits, Churchill was keeping morale high in Britain and keeping the Germans guessing on any successes they achieved. People in the East End of London at the time spoke of the deafening sound as the rocket landed and exploded in the residential area. Houses crashed to the ground with the inhabitants trapped inside. The rockets tended to be sent over at night when most people were in bed. Many houses were badly damaged. The craters made were thirty feet wide and eight or nine feet deep. It only took around five minutes from launch in the Netherlands to detonation in England.

Despite its limited success during the war, the V2 was one of the most expensive weapons ever to be made, costing one million Reichsmarks per rocket. However, it was too primitive to be truly effective, in that it could not be guided to a specific target and only detonated once it was imbedded in its target. Yet the technical expertise was used after the war by the British and the Americans who advanced the ideas first pioneered in Germany. They captured many of the scientists and technicians involved in its development, as did the Russians, and thus began an arms race where the Soviet Union went on to develop the Scud missile from the knowledge given to them by the captured technicians and scientists. It was Soviet soldiers who destroyed the facility at Peenemünde after the war but today the former power station, airport and railway are still there in evidence as testament to Hitler's rocket programme.

Prisoner of war Dr Paul Schröder, number A967234, first came to light in a letter from the Ministry of Supply dated 24 April 1946 sent to Mr Potter at the Political Intelligence Department at the Foreign Office in London. In it, Schröder had been held for interrogation purposes at the Armaments Design Department where he was to give 'certain technical information' on his work in Germany. There seems to be a discrepancy with the Intelligence Department and the Design Department, as the former found that he was uncooperative but the latter found 'no fault' with him.

In a separate letter to Lt.-Col. Fraser dated one week later Schröder had been coerced into writing a treatise on his work. The British Government saw him as an expert on 'the technicalities of rocket projectiles' and as such the prisoner was to be treated well until the work was done. Any misdemeanours were to be ignored and kept secret because, according to the letter, 'the work he is producing has been proved by British technicians to be invaluable' and moreover was top secret. This information was unavailable to the German authorities and it was hoped it would give the British advancement for their own missile programmes of the future.

During his time in captivity, Schröder had written down every technical detail about his rocket data, however, in a moment of madness it seems, his attitude had irritated some non-commissioned officers who had angrily destroyed his first draft. With his second draft, he worked closely with the Design Department at the Ministry of Supply in Halstead and the information was invaluable to the British.

The order to ignore any misdemeanours on his part meant Schröder had a relatively free hand. No explanation was to be given to any one as to why he was to be treated so leniently due to the secretive nature of his work. No one needed to know and on no account was it to be explained to the Ministry of Supply or anyone else who decided to ask questions on his treatment.

In October 1946 Schröder found himself in Camp 184 at Llanmartin in Wales. Unhappy at being incarcerated, he wrote a petition to the camp commandant to be forwarded to his superiors. In it he claimed that he was only held as a prisoner because of the uniform he wore when he was captured in the British zone in Germany, but he claimed that he was not a soldier during the war but a 'scientist, I served as a civil servant employed by the German Waffenamt'. His work had only involved scientific research on rocket warfare and in order to escape from the Russians, for whom he did not want to give his expertise, he took up his old rank of lieutenant which he had gained during World War I. He ended up in front of the British in Hamburg and was transported to London by plane on 4 June 1945. There he was interrogated, then placed in a prisoner of war camp until it was decided what to do with him.

On 1 February 1946 he began his work at Halstead, writing down his intimate knowledge of rockets and 'developing a theory of my own' which had been requested by the Department of Armament Design. However, in his petition he complains that under the condition of being a prisoner of war, his work had been 'interrupted' because of his living conditions. He appealed to His Majesty's Government to give him more suitable accommodation to continue the work. It must be remembered that he and the other scientists had at their disposal anything they wanted when they were developing the rocketry science in Germany, and vast sums of money were poured into the project rather than being spent elsewhere on armaments. Hitler had seen the rockets as the answer to all his problems on the front lines. Schröder had been used to having all the necessary equipment on hand and worked in more accommodating surroundings. He had also been a free man.

Schröder had been born in Bayern in 1894. His parents were poor, yet a chance acquaintance with a German American Jew, Mr James Loeb, paid for the young boy's schooling. Loeb's son-in-law also helped Schröder during a period when he was out of work between 1931 and 1936 by allowing him to withdraw money from the Wassermann Bank in Berlin. During World War I Schröder had gained the rank of Oberleutnant in the army. By the outbreak of World War II, he had turned his attention to science. From 1937 to 1942 he had been working at Peenemünde under General-Major Dr Walter Dornberger as Abteilungsleiter, or head of department.

Dornberger himself was now in British hands. He had been captured at Reutte in Germany just days before the Allies declared victory in Europe. He was no stranger to being a prisoner of war, having been in French hands for almost two years at the end of World War I. He became one of Germany's most prominent scientists, having studied physics at university in Charlottenburg where he gained an engineering degree. In 1932 he had been approached by members of Verein für Raumschiffahrt, the Space Flight Society, an amateur group seeking funding to develop a rocket. It was at this time Wernher von Braun joined him in his work. In 1937, he had been transferred to Peenemünde, working with von Braun, where the development of the A series of rocket missiles were being built. With Schröder at his side, Dornberger developed the V2 bomb that caused so much destruction in Britain during World War II, and remained head of the project until 1944 when Heinrich Himmler replaced him.

In November 1942 Schröder went on to become Gruppenleiter [group leader] under Oberstleutnant Krober. For his work, he received the Kriegsverdienstkreuz, the war merit cross, for his scientific achievements during the war. When he first started work at Peenemünde, his basic salary amounted to five hundred Reichmarks a month, rising to nine hundred and ninety-five by the time he had stopped working there. According to Lt.-Col. Scotland of the War Crimes Interrogation Unit in London, if Schröder, as he claimed, was not a Nazi, his true feelings and loyalties were 'kept well-concealed by him, otherwise he could not have been employed there', and he would not have been decorated either, or it seems highly unlikely.

Scotland was sceptical simply because he knew what he was talking about. To be so high up and not be a Nazi was unthinkable yet Schröder protested that he was not. This appears to tie in with the character of Schröder, as he seemed to say one thing, yet do the opposite. Many who interviewed him noted this. If Schröder had failed to show his allegiance to Adolf Hitler, he would never have been allowed to work on such a sensitive project but would have been assigned to other work in the field of his expertise under very different circumstances and surroundings. Peenemünde was a place of top secret work and Schröder was part of that elite group of scientists and technicians.

In a report on him by Captain S. Coffman in November 1946, Schröder had reiterated his claim that when the Russians were advancing, he got himself into a position so that when Germany surrendered he would be able to place himself at the disposal of the British. Dornberger and von Braun both led their staff westwards when the evacuation of the site got underway as the Russians advanced and handed themselves over to mainly American forces. Like many Germans, Schröder hated the Russians. He believed that they were the enemy of all mankind and as they advanced on Berlin, he knew the war was lost so he made sure that he was in a situation where the Russian troops would not capture him and force him to work on their projects and use his expertise. The Nazi regime had indoctrinated many to believe that Bolshevism was the true enemy and that many were Jewish to boot. The propaganda which people had been subjected to made them hate Soviet Russia and all that it stood for, especially after their brutalised attack on Berlin immediately after the fall of Hitler. The Soviet troops had plundered the city, raping its women and hanging its men. This news had spread fast as many fled westward to escape. Yet in the end, the Soviet troops managed to capture many of the scientists and technicians so desperate not to be caught by them but not the elite ones who opted for the Allies as a better option.

During the questioning, the Captain could not get Schröder to commit himself to any political persuasion. On the subject of Hitler and the Nazi regime, he claimed that Hitler was not a criminal and that Nazi policy was only rejected because it failed. Coffman was of the opinion that Schröder 'has a complete lack of appreciation or understanding of the fundamental amorality of the Nazi idea'. What is important here is the insight this gave Coffman. Schröder was condoning the Nazi regime. He is of the opinion that Hitler's policies were not ones that were criminal, but ones that had simply been unsuccessful. Perhaps if the policies had been nurtured, remodelled and adapted as they went along, the regime may have succeeded in all its goals for the German people. Hitler, according to Schröder, had simply made mistakes, and for all the destruction caused by the war, was not, in his eyes, a criminal in any way and he should not have felt guilt when he died in the bunker in Berlin.

On the question of the Treaty of Versailles and the sister treaties of St Germain, Trianon, Neuilly and Sèrves, Schröder believed that they were unnecessary and that the Anschluß of 1938 was not an act of aggression but born out of necessity by both countries. He saw it as a strengthening of the relations between the two states, both politically and economically, and since Hitler was in fact an Austrian, it made sense for the two countries to unite.

Austria, at the end of World War I, was a tiny republican state, borne out of the Treaty of St Germain, but many Austrians had foreseen the problems of economics and the Depression of the 1930s brought about a massive shift in attitude, whereby many realised that if they had been allowed to be part of a Greater Germany, the economy would be on the road to recovery like that of her neighbour. Also apparent was the political unrest in the country due to the many differing parties, whereas Germany seemed to have a grip on its political direction, although Austria did become an almost totalitarian state in the thirties before the Anschluß.

Schröder goes on to say the German people were not responsible for the war but he conceded that they wanted to follow Hitler's lead. This statement can be interpreted two ways. Perhaps Schröder was saying that even though the German people voted Hitler into power and remained faithful to him when in power, they did not expect the war to last so long, or indeed expect war to break out on the scale it did. On the other hand, he could be suggesting that people did not really understand what Hitler was all about. All they saw in him in the immediate future had been a strong leader who was helping them to put the Depression behind them and finding a more affluent lifestyle in a modern Germany. However, all that said, history balances out in much the same way as Schröder that the people were not themselves individually responsible for the war, but the politicians were. But who voted the politicians in? This is a vicious cycle. The army, the navy, the air force, the politicians and the people could all be blamed. On the other hand, they were doing their jobs and indoctrinated by the most powerful propaganda machine ever seen in their country and if they did not do as they were bid, they could have been shot, hanged, beaten or sent off to the camps like so many of their compatriots. There are no clear answers.

Repeatedly Schröder saw himself as a civilian, not as a soldier; however, according to Coffman, who had information from a 'white' prisoner at Camp 403 at Brockley near Bristol who had spent time with Schröder, he had the 'air of militaristic superiority'. Ending his report, the captain considered him to be an opportunist at any given chance and that he would sell himself to the highest bidder if that chance arose. Schröder himself had suggested that if the British did not want his work he could go back to Germany to the American Zone, not the British one, and work for someone else. He was adamant that the British should release him, but he was graded once more as a Category 'C+', which grieved him tremendously as he felt that he should not be judged politically by the British authorities.

In 1947 things were no better for the highly contradictory Dr Schröder. He was to be interrogated by the head of the London District Cage, Lt.-Col. A. P. Scotland. In his covering letter to A. H. Keane of the Segregation Section, Scotland describes Schröder quite simply, that in his opinion he was definitely a Category 'C+' with 'as many pluses as you like. He is a public enemy from our viewpoint'.

On 17 April 1947 Schröder was held in Kensington Palace Gardens at the war Crimes Interrogation Unit. Scotland and his men had many years of experience in interrogation and Schröder was no exception to the rule that he would come away having told Scotland what he wanted to know. He must have been surprised when Scotland spoke to him fluently in his own native tongue. Instantly, Scotland disliked Schröder. When he told his story to him, he skipped pieces of information and it seemed to Scotland like a well rehearsed speech rather than a natural narrative. But Scotland was knowledgeable and picked up on several of the points Schröder makes as being at the least inconceivable and at most downright lies. Being a Nazi at Peenemünde must have been a prerequisite, and it is this point and that of his benefactor in the 1930s that makes Scotland highly suspicious of Schröder's story. Schröder explained to Scotland that he was a civilian and that when he knew Germany had lost the war he bought himself a uniform and had a pay book issued, yet he still drew a salary from Peenemünde by post cheques drawn on Stettin. Scotland noted how clever Schröder was in choosing to put on a uniform: 'The advantage of being in uniform was, of course, that he could have the protection of the Geneva Convention when the war ended'.

According to Scotland's letter, when he left Peenemünde in 1942 and with his chosen version of his background, Schröder could have expected to find himself in a concentration camp, yet by being cunning, his life took a different path. At Scotland's suggestion, he asked that Schröder 'be thoroughly re-vetted and his record should make it impossible for him ever to be completely released from the control of a German Disarmament Commission … therefore from our point of view a 'C+' for the whole of his remaining working years'.

A man simply noted as Mr Wendl wrote his own report on Schröder in August 1947 when Schröder was at Camp 165: this backed earlier claims of the difficulty in forming a definitive opinion of the man. He was found to be very difficult to work with and had a very high opinion of himself according to Wendl. Although not politically easily categorised, Wendl plumps for him being conservative. He also notes that he is very strongly anti-Communist and very anti-Labour government. When General Robertson gave a speech suggesting that the German technicians must be prevented from doing their 'devilish work', Schröder replied to his British colleagues that 'I trust my work is no longer devilish'. He was also furious at the Government for believing that anyone who worked at Peenemünde must have been a Nazi.

Wendl notes that Schröder had spent most of his career working with the technical problems involved in armaments and this in itself caused his political grading to be troublesome. Wendl wrote that Schröder did understand that his grading would not change, and that at Watten he would be one of the very last to be repatriated and would be a civilian internee. Schröder told Wendl that the Americans knew where he was being held and that they would take him to the United States for him to work for them. He was committed, if nothing else, to his work. As a compromise, Wendl suggested handing Schröder over to the Americans so he could have his time 'to fill the centre stage and also retain something of the faith which he still apparently places in the goodwill of this country'. A stark warning from Wendl suggested that if no solution was found to the Schröder problem, he would definitely have to be interned for the rest of his life. He was a difficult man to like who in any case showed the antagonism of the 'Prussian manner' so easily conferred upon him by the British. He was seen as an 'opportunist of the first order' but was not the 'big shot as he likes to think'.

It is not known what happened to Schröder after his captivity and subsequent release. As for others who worked on the V1 and V2 rockets, Dornberger was held by the British for two years, but never stood trial as a war criminal. This was because he claimed that the V2 was never intended to be launched against civilian targets, only military ones, and said that it was only after the SS under Heinrich Himmler took over the project that civilians were seen as fair game by the hierarchy. When Himmler had removed him, Albert Speer, the high-ranking Nazi architect who had influence in the inner circle of the Reich administration, managed to transfer Dornberger and his staff onto another project. This involved work on anti-bomber defences, although his replacement on the V2 project, Kammler, made this as awkward as he possibly could for Dornberger. On his release, Dornberger emigrated to the United States of America and worked for the US Air Force on guided missile projects. For fifteen years until 1965, he worked for the Bell Aircraft Corporation and wrote a book on his time working on the V2. He returned to Germany where he died in 1980 aged 84.

Wernher von Braun surrendered to the American forces and he and his colleagues ended up in Fort Bliss in Texas, where they taught the Americans all about the V2 and rocketry science. In 1950 the group were moved to Alabama, which was to become his home for twenty years, and he became a US citizen in 1955. In 1960 the Marshall Space Flight Center opened in Huntsville, part of the young NASA organisation, with the object of landing a man on the moon. Von Braun's expertise was directly involved in the Saturn V rocket that launched the Apollo 11 in July 1969. He retired from NASA in 1972. However, his career was far from over, as he became involved in the establishment of what went on to become the National Space Society, and became Chief Executive Officer of OTRAG, a German company involved in the development of an alternative system of propulsion rockets. In 1976, von Braun discovered he had cancer. In June the following year he died aged 65.

Chapter 9

Aid to Hitler

———

The camp at Watten held an array of German hierarchy. One such person was at one time Adolf Hitler's personal aid, SS-Obersturmbannführer Max Wünsche who was held in the camp in 1947.

Wünsche was born on 20 April 1915 in the Saxony town of Kittlitz, son of a forester. After completing primary schooling, he attended the secondary school in Bautzen in eastern Saxony then went on into further education. In 1928 he joined the Reichslandbund, which was an agricultural trade union, at the same time as he attended college. He found work at an accountancy firm when he finished his studies and eventually became head of the department. By November 1932 Wünsche had joined the Hitlerjugend and less than a year later had joined the SS in July 1933. He attended a five-month training course in Jüterbog in the Teltow-Fläming district of Brandenburg so he could become a non-commissioned officer, which he duly completed, and decided to become a fully-fledged officer. He attended SS-Junkerschule, a school dedicated to the training of Waffen-SS officers under a strict military regime, at Bad Tölz in Bavaria. It took another two years of training before he graduated.

On his birthday in 1936 he received what he saw as a wonderful present; he was commissioned and promoted to SS-Untersturmführer and was assigned to the Leibstandarte as Zugführer, or platoon leader, in 9 Kompanie. He was soon reassigned to 17 Kompanie, where he remained until 1 October 1938. It was at this time Wünsche was transferred to become part of the Begeleitkommando des Führers. This was Hitler's personal escort detachment and the closest Wünsche would ever be to the Führer. His title was Orderly Officer, but his role changed and he became Hitler's adjutant or butler. He remained in the post until early 1940. As adjutant, Wünsche liaised with the armed forces and organised meetings, took minutes and kept a diary for the Führer. He dealt with correspondence and did some administrative work. He also accompanied Hitler to many functions and acted partly as a personal bodyguard.

Many photographs of Hitler during 1938 to early 1940 show the young Wünsche in the background. One famous photograph was taken at a girls' school in 1938 and the white-

Max Wünsche, Hitler's one-time adjutant, was highly regarded in the inner circles of the Third Reich.

uniformed Wünsche is at Hitler's side. Both are smiling broadly as they joked with the girls. Other photographs show him hovering in the background during parades as he was never far from the Führer at that time. During the Anschluß celebrations in Vienna in 1938, Wünsche stood next to Hitler when he gave his speech, and after the Fall of France he was seen on the balcony with Hitler and Hermann Göring. Wünsche is also pictured at a party to celebrate the New Year in 1938–9.

In early 1940 Wünsche was transferred back to the Leibstandarte as commander of the 2 Zug in15 Kradschützenkompanie which was directly under the command of Kurt 'Panzermeyer' Meyer, who later went on to become an SS-Brigadefürher. Wünsche took part in the invasion of France and the Low Countries before being sent back to the Begleitkommando des Führers on 1 of June 1940. During his time in France, Wünsche had close contact with Josef 'Sepp'

Dietrich, the latter being later interrogated in London by Lt.-Col. Scotland at the London District Cage about an incident involving captured British troops. It is unknown whether Wünsche was interrogated about the same incident while he was incarcerated at Watten.

In May 1940, at Wormhoudt in northern France, the Leibstandarte came under fire from the 2nd Royal Warwickshire Regiment, who were supported by the Cheshires with their machine-gun armoury. The Germans had hoped to cut off the retreating British troops at Dunkirk, but the British put up strong resistance. Traps had been set for the Germans by several sections of the British guard, but nonetheless they eventually lost the battle. The British, however, had managed to blow up Dietrich's car, which had, it is thought, Max Wünsche as a passenger. The car had burst into flames, with huge plumes of smoke billowing into the sky, yet remarkably the two men escaped. The driver however was killed. The two men crawled into a ditch and waited for around five hours before they were rescued.

By this time, though, the SS troops thought that their commanding officer had run into a trap and had subsequently died, so they pressed on. Captain Wilhelm Mohnke took over as battalion commander and that was when the treatment of the captured British soldiers changed dramatically. Around three hundred and thirty British prisoners were taken, eighty of them by Mohnke's 2nd Battalion. The men were interrogated and taken to the security of a prison camp but on seeing the men marching along the road, Mohnke was furious. He had given strict orders not to take them as prisoners so he ordered guards to escort the eighty men his battalion had captured along a farm track to a barn about a mile away. Those who fell were shot or prodded with bayonets to make them walk faster. Captain Allen protested when the men were faced with going into the barn. He knew what was about to happen, but they were forced inside. Grenades were thrown in then rifle fire peppered the barn. Allen managed to escape with another man, but he was fatally wounded. The other soldier survived by crawling to a nearby farmhouse.

Those who had survived in the barn were ordered outside in groups of five at a time. The confused men did as they were instructed, with the sounds of prayers being said by those left behind. As they alighted from the barn, they were met by five Germans with their rifles at the ready. The officer in charge counted out 'Ein'. There was a hail of fire and one man dropped. 'Zwei', and another man fell and so it went on until all five lay dead. The next group were called out and the same scenario took place. When it was finally over, there were few survivors, and those who did lay for as long as they possibly could in case the soldiers returned and finished them off.

However, the Germans soon realised that this method was too time consuming and returned to the barn, opening fire, spraying it with bullets. Only when they were convinced that all the men were dead did they stop firing. Slowly, after quite some time had passed, the survivors began to move, many of them suffering horrendous wounds, but they had only saved their own lives by acting dead. Some of the early survivors, however, died overnight in the barn. In all, only fifteen of the eighty men herded into the barn that day survived.

The German soldiers left the scene at the barn and scoured the local village. When they found escaped British troops, they killed them by shooting them, stabbing them or simply clubbing them to death.

A few days later, soldiers of the Wehrmacht passed nearby and the surviving men called out to them for help. They came and dressed the wounds of the men and gave them clean water to drink. When the British told the German soldiers what had happened, about being captured by the Waffen-SS then being shot because they did not want to be bogged down with prisoners of war during their rapid advance, the Germans were horrified. Although the British survivors were taken as prisoners of war, they were treated by medics and helped by the Wehrmacht.

As for Wünsche and Dietrich, they had walked away unscathed. By later that same day, Dietrich was back in his office demanding a report on the day's events. When he heard of the killings at Wormhoudt, he immediately invoked the SS oath. Everyone present was sworn to secrecy. Mohnke was interrogated after the war but there was not enough evidence to bring him to trial, even though British investigations have numerous accounts of what happened from local villagers, and the men who survived. Mohnke was also charged in connection with the murder of three Canadian soldiers, Ionkel, Benner and Owens, after they had been interrogated by him on 11 June 1944. He had been captured by the Russians and was held by them until 1955, even though efforts had been made by the British for his extradition. He worked in Germany selling tucks and died in 2001, aged ninety.

After Wünsche's return to the Begleitkommando des Führers in June 1940, there were rumours of a scandal involving Wünsche and the treatment of guests at Berghof. The outcome was his dismissal, although his close friend and ally Martin Bormann, Hitler's private secretary, tried to help him, though to no avail. Wünsche was sent on his way, back to Leibstandarte SS Adolf Hitler. He had become adjutant to 'Sepp' Dietrich.

Joesef 'Sepp' Dietrich had an illustrious career to date when Wünsche joined him. Born in Bavaria in 1892, he had served as a paymaster-sergeant and in the tanks troops before joining the *Freikorps* fighting against the Munich Soviet Republic. He joined the Nazi party in 1928 and steadily rose through the ranks after Hitler gained power. Under Hitler's orders, he took part in the Night of the Long Knives in 1934 and executed many members of the SA, the Sturmabteilung, or stormtroopers. For his troubles he was promoted to SS-Obergruppenführer and made General der Waffen-SS in 1940. By this time, he had received numerous awards, including the Knights Cross, Anschluß Medal, and a Clasp to the Iron Cross Second and First Classes. Later he would go on to receive the Knights Cross with Oak Leaves, Swords and Diamonds, the highest accolade given by the Third Reich. He had also made inroads in the campaign on the Western Front, having taken part at Dunkirk, forcing the Allies back to the beach to be evacuated, and in the advance on Paris.

Wünsche served with Dietrich in the Balkan Campaign, when they fought in Greece and Yugoslavia. This latter campaign began in April 1941 with the invasion by Italian and German troops after the Serbian population became deeply unhappy with the Prince Regent joining the Axis powers in the Tripartite Pact, following in the footsteps of Hungary, Romania and Bulgaria. The Axis armies converged on the capital from three different approaches while the Luftwaffe bombed Belgrade into submission and it took only eleven days until Yugoslavia admitted defeat and surrendered. Germany lost less than one hundred and sixty men. Hitler needed these Balkan states in the Axis simply to bolster the Axis numbers, especially after Italy's defeat at the hands of Greece in 1940 but also, Romania had large oilfields, which were crucial to the German economy. He thought the United Kingdom would bomb the oilfields and therefore have a stranglehold over Germany's fuel supply for her army on the front lines. In Greece, in April of the same year, the Germans invaded via Bulgaria with the Leibstandarte SS Adolf Hitler, advancing south to occupy the town of Vevi on 11 April. At Metsovon Pass a week later, the LSSAH fought a ferocious battle with several Greek units but they had the advantage of more equipment. On 20 April, 'Sepp' Dietrich was asked to accept the surrender of Greek troops but the document for the acceptance of surrender was not signed until three days later at Mussolini's insistence that the Italians be involved in it. Athens fell on 27 April, outnumbered by German and Axis troops. This caused friction between Hitler and Stalin over their sphere of influence in the region. Later, Wünsche and Dietrich both went on to be part of Operation Barbarossa, the invasion of Russia in June 1941.

Barbarossa was the largest single military operation of all time, beating Operation Overlord, which took place in Normandy three years later. Over three million German troops were deployed. Hitler had ordered his troops in December 1940 to crush the Russians in a quick campaign, and by May 1941 the treatment of the enemy was encapsulated in an order signed by Generalfeldmarschall Keitel, although he had severe reservations about the invasion and had tendered his resignation over it. Hitler had refused and Keitel capitulated. The ruthlessness is tangible. The enemy fighters were to be mercilessly disposed of by the military regardless of whether they were surrendering or not and permission was given for the soldiers to act callously if they felt in any way threatened by the civilian population. It was a blank cheque for brutality.

The distances involved and the use of captured enemy vehicles compounded the problems facing the troops as Barbarossa got underway. Old peasant carts were attached to horses, which pulled the equipment for the Panzer groups. There were three different groups involved; the Panzers of Army Group North, Panzers of Army Group Centre and Panzers of Army Group South. Wünsche was attached to this latter group, which met fierce resistance in the first week of the invasion but as they moved south over the difficult terrain of the Pripet Marshes, they found that the lands of the Ukraine were well-suited to tanks. According to Wünsche's later adjutant, Hauptsturmführer Georg Isecke, another of Watten's prisoners of war, Wünsche took the opportunity to fly sorties in a Fiesler Storch to check out the enemy positions. The Storch had first been used in 1936 and continued until the end of the war. It was a fabric-covered, high-winged monoplane, used mainly for observation purposes, and could take off in very light winds from ground of just over 60 metres (roughly 200 feet) and it could land within a stretch of ground of only 20 metres (roughly 65 feet). Its maximum speed reached over 100 miles per hour, thanks to its 240 horsepower, eight-cylinder inverted-V engine, with a maximum range of 239 miles. Its wingspan was 14 metres (over 45 feet) with a body length of 9.75 metres (roughly 31 feet). For defence, the Storch was fitted with a rear-firing machine gun on a pivot mount to deter any enemy that got too close. Wünsche's sorties paid dividends, most significantly when in late July, the Germans pushed into Novo-Archangelsk, trapping Russian troops. Flying the Storch was not, however, without its risks. Theodor Eicke, the father of the concentration camp movement, was shot down flying in one on a reconnaissance mission shortly after being promoted to Obergruppenführer during the opening stages of the Third

Battle of Kharkov. 'Sepp' Dietrich too flew sorties and was awarded the Pilot Observer Badge in Gold with Diamonds by Herman Göring.

As the troops made deeper inroads into the southern fringes of Russia they soon reached the Crimea where Wünsche deputised on two separate occasions for the divisional commander, SS-Hauptsturmführer Wilhelm Keilhaus, who himself was deputised by SS Hauptsturmführer Rudolf Lehmann. Wünsche also took over when the Germans fought at Berdjansk, Mariupol and Taganrog, when he commanded various sub-units following the deaths of their commanders, and he met with some degree of success. All of these cities were important strategically as they sat on the Sea of Azov, a northern part of the Black Sea in the Ukraine, and were some of the most significant seaports in the region.

Fighting on in the Russian campaign, Wünsche's men managed to stop the Soviet troops breaking through German lines. In June 1942 Wünsche left the Russian Front and returned to Berlin to the Kriegschule to undertake a three-month training course to become a member of the General Staff. This he successfully completed and was promoted to SS-Sturmbannführer. By October he had taken command of the I. Abteilung in the newly-formed Panzerregiment. This regiment was to see Wünsche fight at the battle of Kharkov.

That same month, Hitler had issued orders to all commanding officers on the Eastern Front. They were to 'exterminate … enemy sabotage parties' and referred back to the 'ruthless brutality' which brought the soldiers success earlier in the campaign which allowed the supplies to reach those on the fighting front. Any soldier who did not apply this ruthless action was to be 'reported without pity or … immediately to be called severely to account'. Any man found so guilty 'is to be shot immediately after their interrogation'.

Fighting through the atrocious Russian winter weather, the I. Abteilung inflicted massive losses on the hitherto unstoppable Russian advance at the city of Merefa in the eastern Ukraine. Their goal was to reach Kurt 'Panzermeyer' Meyer and his men who had been encircled and were in danger of being wiped out. Over a number of days, thanks to Wünsche's leadership, they reached Meyer as they smashed their way through enemy lines, opening up the supply and communication lines for the trapped Germans. The journey to save Meyer and his men had been difficult. The snow lay several feet deep and the freezing temperatures and rough terrain did not in any way help the Germans. Meyer and Wünsche's men joined forces, forming a Kampfgruppe and carried forward, their ultimate goal still being Kharkov.

By using his own initiative, Wünsche ordered his men to encircle the Russians at Jeremejwka, which led to one of his greatest successes. Fifty-four heavy guns were destroyed and over nine hundred Russian troops lay injured or dead on the battlefield. For this action, Wünsche received the Knight's Cross in Gold on 28 February 1943. Two weeks later Kharkov, also known as Kharkiv, was taken. By the time the city was liberated by the Red Army on 23 August 1943, under Operation Polovdets Rumyantsev, much of it had been destroyed and many of its inhabitants had been killed. The operation to free the city had begun in early August and the Germans were pushed back at an astonishing rate. It was the beginning of a concerted effort by the Soviet Red Army to push the Wehrmacht out of their sphere of influence.

However, in June 1943, Wünsche was yet again rewarded for his successes in the east. A new division was being formed which Wünsche, along with SS-Brigadeführer Fritz Witt, was given command of the 12 SS-Panzerdivision *Hitlerjugend* was formed and Wünsche was to see action in the west along with Kurt Meyer once more. Originally it was to have the title Panzergrenadier, but it was renamed following on from the fact that it was to be a Panzer unit. This Panzerdivision was about to become the most famous in Germany.

In the spring of 1944 the 12 SS-Panzerdivision *Hitlerjugend* began training around the French town of Caen. This was a move that was to prove fruitful, for by early June the soldiers knew the terrain well and were ready for combat. With around two hundred tanks, some tank destroyers and flak guns, they were as well-prepared as they could be for any military action.

At dawn on 6 June 1944, Operations Neptune and Overlord unfolded on the beaches of Normandy. The British and their allies launched the massive attack to begin the fight to free Europe from Nazi domination. They sought to secure the beachhead and began the push inland. However, as the British and Canadian forces made inroads, they met with fierce resistance by the 12 SS-Panzerdivision, with its youthful morale kept high by Wünsche. Meyer had set up a command post at Abbey Ardenne which made it easy for him to see the advancing troops. Wünsche, as commander of the tank regiment, was given the order to attack. Near Franqueville, the British tanks began to be hit and exploded, with the men jumping from the burning vehicles. It is thought that it was at this time Meyer gave the order that no prisoners be taken. This meant they were to be shot, and later he was to stand trial for the murder of eighteen Canadian troops who had been killed in this manner.

On 8 June Wünsche sustained a head wound when fighting broke out around the Bretteville-l'Orgueilleuse area when the Germans launched an attack on the Canadians from the east. During the numerous engagements, Wünsche and his men destroyed nearly two hundred and twenty allied tanks in their bid to keep the enemy at bay. For this, he was awarded the Oak Leaves. However, the Allies were stubborn and resolute. As the advance took hold, losses on the German side became much heavier, including the death of SS-Brigadeführer Witt, on 14 June, when he was hit by a volley of British gunfire directed at his command post. Meyer took charge and became the youngest divisional commander during the war. In August, the Allied troops had surrounded the Germans at the Falaise gap. Wünsche had managed to keep the gap open to allow his troops to escape; however, this was soon plugged by the Allied forces. Wünsche, Isecke (his adjutant) and a couple of others managed to escape. Isecke somehow became separated from the group and was captured four days later by the British. Wünsche and a comrade who had managed to stay with him found a German vehicle and drove to St Lambert, where the Canadians held a strong position. The two men hid in bushes until nightfall. However, Wünsche and his comrade were soon in the hands of the Allies as prisoners of war. Meyer escaped until his capture in September in Belgium. He had been promoted to SS-Brigadeführer, given Swords to add to the Knights Cross with Oak Leaves but was now in American hands.

With his wartime career now over, Wünsche still had a distinguished list of awards, including the Iron Cross I, awarded in 1940, the Eastern Front Medal in 1942, the German Cross in Gold in 1943 and the Knight's Cross in 1943. He had worked hard and risen from being an SS-Obersturmführer in 1938, SS-Hauptsturmführer in 1940, SS-Sturmbannführer in 1942 to finally SS-Obersturmbannführer in 1944.

After spending time in various other prisoner of war camps, Wünsche and Isecke ended up at Watten in 1947. Wünsche was given the prisoner of war number A938670 and classed as a category 'C+', while his adjutant, Georg Isecke was also classed as a 'C+' prisoner. Both men were held at Watten until the camp's closure in 1948.

In a letter dated 7 November 1947, a call was made to the Repatriation Desk at the Foreign Office in London from the head of Featherstone Park Camp at Haltwhistle in Northumberland. It requested the return of four prisoners held at Watten, including Gunter d'Alquen and Max Wünsche. The captain ended the letter that he would be very much obliged if these men would be returned as 'believe it or not: they deserve it'. He claimed that these men were not 'suitable' for Camp 165 as they were considered 'blacks' and Camp 165 was beginning its shutdown.

Wünsche was finally released by the British in 1948 having been in their hands for four years. He returned to Germany, settling down eventually in Munich and taking on the role of manager of an industrial plant in Wuppertal. He was married to Ingeborg and had a family. He doted on his children. He kept a low profile for the rest of his life, although he did remain firm friends with Kurt Meyer and 'Sepp' Dietrich. In 1956, another friend, Joachin Peiper, was released from prison and the four men celebrated together. Dietrich had already served time for his part in the Malmedy massacre in Belgium in December 1944, where he ordered the execution of American prisoners of war, but on his release, he was re-arrested and in 1957 sentenced to nineteen months for his part in the Night of the Long Knives. He was released in early 1959 due to poor health. Later, Wünsche attended the funerals of Meyer and Dietrich, the latter dying in 1966 from a heart attack. At his funeral, over six thousand of his former colleagues turned up including Wünsche. But Wünsche was reluctant to ever be photographed with any of them. He retired in 1980.

Due to his actions and his ranking, postwar life was, however, made difficult for Max Wünsche. His life was allegedly put in danger by threats made by left-wing fanatics and it is thought that when he went to work he had two bodyguards by his side. He died on 17 April 1995, three days short of his eighty-first birthday, after a long illness.

Hitler and Wünsche had shared the same birthday and each year, Wünsche contacted Hitler to wish him well. In April 1944, Wünsche was at Berghof, one of the guests of Hitler, along with 'Sepp' Dietrich and SS Chief Heinrich Himmler. It was Hitler's fifty-fifth birthday and the young Wünsche, part of the Leibstandarte, congratulated him. Having been Hitler's one-time adjutant, the two men knew each other and were always cordial and friendly towards one another. It was rumoured that when Hitler heard that Wünsche had been captured at Falaise, he suggested an exchange of British prisoners of war for his former aid but this never happened. The wife of Martin Bormann, Hitler's secretary, apparently became extremely upset when she had wrongly been told Wünsche had died during the Russian campaign. He was highly regarded and well-liked in the inner circles of the Third Reich.

Chapter 10

U-Boat Hero

The U-boat campaign in the Atlantic was the ultimate weapon in Hitler's war. During the 1930s he had amassed a war machine by means diplomatic and other. Versailles had been torn apart and, by 1939, Germany had a military presence not seen in twenty years. The U-boat fleet had been born once more and one of its most notable commanders was eventually held at Watten. At the outbreak of war, Germany had seventy U-boats available for action. By less than two years later it was estimated she had only twenty left.

On 1 May 1912 in Heidau in Silesia, Germany, Otto Kretschmer was born, son of a school-teacher. By the age of seventeen Kretschmer already knew what his chosen career path would be, but for eight months he spent time in Exeter where he learned to speak English fluently. A year later he began his naval career by joining the Kriegsmarine in April 1930. Although in its infancy, the Weimar Republic had begun to expand the navy and young men like Kretschmer were welcomed by the admiralty. After completing three months of officer-training plus time on the training ship *Niobe*, he gained the rank of Seekadett and served on the *Deutschland* and the cruiser *Emden* but his career path changed when the opportunity arose for him to join the submarine fleet in 1936 at Kiel. Among his contemporaries were Gunter Prien and Joachim Schepke, but the young Kretschmer stood out. He had a thirst for knowledge about the sea and a determination that dwarfed that of other recruits. His reputation was also beginning to form. He would not tolerate weakness of any kind from other men and if they did not work to his high standards they were often shown contempt. However, he did have another side to him that provided the men with the opportunity to laugh, but it was always on his own terms.

That same year, on 1 June, the young Kretschmer was promoted to Oberleutnant zur See and a year later he was given his first command of U-35, which saw him taking part in the Spanish Civil War. U-35 was to patrol the Spanish coast in order to protect Franco's interests, and after sinking no shipping whatsoever, returned to Germany after less than a month at sea. In September 1937 Kretschmer was re-assigned to take command of U-23 and when war broke out in 1939 he remained at its helm.

By early 1940 Kretschmer had patrolled the northern fringes of the United Kingdom mainland, laying mines in the Moray Firth off the Scottish east coast. Having laid just nine mines, he got his first of many successes. In January 1940, the Danish tanker *Danmark* was sunk. A month later, the British destroyer HMS *Daring* suffered the same fate in the Pentland Firth on the north coast as she escorted convoy HN-12 from Norway. Kretschmer's destruction of *Daring* was seen as being skilfully carried out and he joined the ranks of only a very few who had sunk enemy warships.

In April 1940 after doing eight patrols, Kretschmer was transferred to a new type of U-boat, termed the Type VIIB, and it was given the number U-99. He had spent two months training at Kiel and finally in June 1940 took to the waters. It was in this U-boat that he became infamous. By December 1940 he had sunk three British merchant cruisers. These were the *Laurentic*, at a tonnage of over 18,000 tons, the *Patroclus* at just over 11,000 tons and the *Forfar* at approximately 16,500 tons. The first two ships had gone to the aid of another, the British freighter *Casanare*, which U-99 had severely damaged off the coast of Ireland in November. The *Forfar* was sunk in early December as it helped to escort Convoy OB-251. Due to the amount of tonnage sunk, Otto Kretschmer earned his place in history as the U-boat ace of World War II. This record of sinking 46,000 gross tons was never surpassed during the war, even though Kretschmer became a prisoner of war in 1941.

During his last patrol in March 1941 he sank another ten ships, however, on 17 March the British had mounted a counter attack. Depth charges were dropped from the British destroyer HMS *Walker*, disabling U-99 and she surfaced off the south-east coast of Iceland, badly damaged. Instead of the U-boat being captured, Otto Kretschmer had it scuttled just after 0330, losing three of his crew. Forty survived. The British captured Kretschmer and the remaining men and it was the beginning of nearly seven years of captivity. During this same battle, his fellow submariner Joachim Schepke was killed. Only sixteen days before hand, Kretschmer had been promoted to Korvettenkapitän.

During his career he had been rewarded for his hard endeavours. In October 1939 he had been awarded the Iron Cross 2nd Class, followed a few weeks later by the U-boat War Badge. Before Christmas that year, he had been given the Iron Cross 1st Class and in August 1940 the Knights Cross. Two months later, he was awarded the Knights Cross with Oak Leaves. The Chancellor, Adolf Hitler, decorated him personally with the Cross in November 1940 in Berlin. And whilst in captivity, on 26th December 1941, his final decoration was awarded, Knights Cross with Oak Leaves and Swords.

Back home in Germany, information about the loss of the two U-boats in March 1941 had reached the German Wehrmacht. On 20 March the boats and their crews were assumed lost in enemy action in the North Atlantic.

In Britain, the heroism seen in Germany was the complete opposite. The Admiralty issued a communiqué on 8 April 1941 to the effect that the U-boat fleet was gaining strength in numbers, but that British countermeasures were beginning to have an effect and successes were being recorded. It goes on to say that the number of U-boat men lost had been significant, and in many cases all men had been lost; however, at that time, the British had over fifty German officers and over four hundred U-boat petty officers and men in captivity, among

Otto Kretschmer — 'the Wolf of the Atlantic'.

them U-boat commander Otto Kretschmer. In Germany, Kretschmer was seen as a hero of the Third Reich because of his notable successes. He was a huge loss to the Kriegsmarine.

On 20 April the First Lord of the Admiralty, Mr A. V. Alexander, announced the death of Schepke to the British public and the capture of Kretschmer. In his statement he said 'I do not think this sort of news will encourage them much'. However, back in Germany, the press had announced that Kretschmer was taking a well-earned break in a Bavarian mountain resort after 'amazing exploits against British merchant shipping'. Alexander was right when he said 'he was known and idolised in Germany as "the Wolf of the Atlantic".'

Alexander went on to mention the death of Schepke and takes great delight in adding that 'I am told that there were only three German U-boat captains who held [Oak Leaves]. Now two out of these three are out of commission ... The German U-boat service is dependant upon the efforts of a few aces and there is cause for gratification in the removal from the trade route of scourges of this sort'.

The First Lord continued that the German fleet had a fight on its hands, with the introduction of more 'escorting destroyers and corvettes expands ... the toll of the enemy will increase until the Battle of the Atlantic is won'.

By late May 1941 it was reported in an official German communiqué that the third one of the trio, Günther Prien, had also been lost as he had not returned from his last expedition. Prien was the other commander to have received the high honour of the Oak Leaves. He had the notable tag of being the hero who had sunk HMS *Royal Oak* in Scapa Flow on the night of 14 October 1939 with the loss of over 800 lives.

After his capture, Otto Kretschmer and his surviving crew members were taken on board the destroyer HMS *Walker*. Soaked, the men were told to strip and were given dry clothes. The opposing crew members found that they had been serving on the Spanish coast at the same time and swapped stories. Kretschmer, meantime, had spent time being question by the ship's commander, Donald Macintyre. Macintyre had been congratulated by Kretschmer and he had thanked him for picking up his men, but needless to say, he was held captive away from his men with an armed guard outside. On one occasion on board, he joined in a game of bridge that continued into the wee small hours. After three days on the ship, they finally docked in Liverpool. The German crew thanked their British counterparts, who in turn warned them that when they were handed over to the army, they might not be treated so well. As Kretschmer walked down the gangway, his men stood to attention in a final salute to their commander as he was driven away to Walton prison. Here, Kretschmer was again kept separate from the crew of U-99, in a small cell, until he was transferred to the London District Cage for interrogation. A few weeks later, Kretschmer found himself in the north of England at Grizedale Hall, Camp 1. At the end of May 1942 he was told that the men in the camp were to be transferred. He was sent to Canada to Camp Bowmanville, also known as Camp 30. Camp Bowmanville was situated roughly eighty kilometres from Toronto on Lake Ontario. It was here that the determined Kretschmer hatched a plan to escape Canada and return to Germany in Operation Kiebitz.

In the autumn of 1942, Kretschmer, who was now the senior camp officer, hatched his plan that would allow four of the inmates, including himself, to escape captivity. He had managed to acquire a two-way radio link with Oberkommando der Marine, the German Naval High Command. The idea was to escape and walk on foot to the eastern seaboard at Pointe Maisonette in New Brunswick, where the men could be picked up by a German U-boat sent by Admiral Dönitz, the Commander-in-Chief of the submarine fleet. It was calculated that it would take the men only four days to reach the bay if conditions were favourable, but crucial to their plan was Dönitz giving his consent to such a scheme. By way of communicating with Dönitz, coded letters were sent via his secretary and because of Kretschmer's reputation, Dönitz replied, giving his consent to the plan. This spurred the men into action. Over the next few months, tunnels were dug long enough for the men to escape well away from the camp, although two of the three were abandoned before completion. One hundred and fifty men took turns at digging out the soil, day and night, while others prepared false identification papers and managed to acquire civilian clothing.

By August 1943 Kretschmer received information that a U-boat would be on patrol during late September, which would surface every two hours for two weeks. This was their chance but they had only limited time to get to Chaleur Bay. Radio communication and further instructions via the coded letters set a date when U-536, under the command of Lieutenant Schauenburg, would be able to rescue them.

With less than a week to go, their plans came crashing down, literally, around them. The men had hidden the soil from the tunnels in the ceiling of their barracks and the sheer weight brought the ceiling down, alerting the Canadian guards. It did not help when one of the prisoners who was tending to a flower patch near the fence fell into the mouth of the tunnel the men had planned to use.

These events alone did not foil the plan. The Canadian intelligence services were well aware of the plot. The Royal Canadian Mounted Police as well as Canadian Military Intelligence had managed to intercept and decode the messages between the prisoners and the German Admiralty. Added to this was a suspect package that had been sent to one of the men. It was opened up by the authorities and inside was a map of a rescue operation planned for New Brunswick. Surveillance began by strategically placing microphones where they heard the sounds of the digging of the tunnels. The intention was to allow the prisoners to get so far then capture them.

When Kretschmer's plan was foiled, another U-boat man, Kapitänleutnant Wolfgang Heyda, proposed a new one. The outcome of this was successful. He escaped from Camp 30, having managed to catapult himself over the fencing, and a number of days later, safely arrived at the rendezvous point in New Brunswick. However, on reaching Pointe Maisonette, Heyda was captured and returned to Bowmanville by the Royal Canadian Military Police, where three days later he informed Kretschmer and the others of the foiled plan.

Meanwhile, preparations were well underway on the German side of things. Schauenburg had been given his orders to pick up the four escaped U-boat captives at Pointe Maisonette; however, he was to tell his crew nothing about the operation until they had arrived off the Canadian coast. U-536 was on her way.

Schauenburg, having reached the Bay of Biscay, received the order to begin Operation Kiebitz on 12 September 1943. He reached Canada four days later and waited as instructed at Chaleur Bay for signals from the escaped prisoners. This was to take place on 26 September.

But by 27 September the U-boat had received no signal from the shoreline. The Canadians by this time were sending down depth charges and hit the U-boat, but Schauenburg decided to wait for the bombardment to stop before he surfaced. Two days passed and the submarine became entangled in some fishing nets which led to debris being twisted round the conning tower. At nightfall the U-boat surfaced but was spotted. Eventually, it managed to escape the bay but the men on board were now becoming ill due to the changes being experienced in the pressure. Schauenburg needed to surface – and soon. After travelling for hundreds of miles, she finally did surface.

On 5 October Schauenburg informed the German Admiralty that Operation Kiebitz had failed and that the U-boat men were still incarcerated in Canada. Six weeks later, U-536 ended up at the bottom of the sea, sunk by the Allies.

Kretschmer was not only involved in Kiebitz. In October 1942, he and others caused what later became known as the Battle of Bowmanville. The commandant of Camp 30, Lt.-Col. James Taylor asked for German prisoners of war to volunteer to be shackled. The senior German officers of the army, air force and submariners refused and at the time for roll-call, none of the prisoners appeared. Calling for back up, Taylor called on his men to shackle one hundred German officers. In the large kitchen of the camp, Kretschmer set up resistance headquarters and the men, numbering around one hundred and fifty, armed themselves with whatever they could find, including iron bars and table legs. The Canadians armed themselves with only baseball bats and had no chance of ending the siege. However, on 10 October the real battle of wills began. The Germans barricaded the kitchen as they were rushed by the Canadian guards, but the Canadians pulled back when they failed to make any headway. The prisoners exited, brandishing their bars. The Canadians counterattacked with high-pressure water hoses and at six in the evening the prisoners surrendered, being unable to defend themselves from the perpetual bombardment from the hoses. The prisoners who had barricaded themselves in the basement of one of the houses, exited after the basement filled up with water, and as a humiliating gesture of power, the Canadian, Lieutenant Brent, hit each man with his cane.

The shackles question arose once more and was again refused and the prisoners returned to their barracks. In the early hours of the following morning, shots were fired at two prisoners attempting to escape, but they were quickly recaptured. Kretschmer advised the guard that if Brent went into the camp, the ill feeling between him and the prisoners would be unbearable and said it would be best if he stayed away. However, Brent entered the compound and word soon spread around the prisoners. As Brent passed the incensed Kretschmer, the young U-boat ace punched him and he fell to the ground. Brent was dragged to House 4, and Kretschmer ordered one of his colleagues from U-99, Volkmar König, to tie him up. He was then marched to the gate when rifle fire broke out. The prisoners dived for cover, although König was wounded, and Brent made it to the gate.

The following morning the barracks were stormed by troops from Barriefield and Kingston. Kretschmer and his men armed themselves with whatever they could find, including bricks to throw from the roofs of the barracks. By early evening, after a battle of attrition, it was over. Many had been wounded on both sides. Around a hundred German officers were marched off in handcuffs while the Canadian soldiers helped themselves to the Germans' belongings as an act of retribution. Among the things taken was Kretschmer's Knight's Cross, which was never recovered.

Kretschmer escaped punishment for the attack on Brent. Instead, another of Watten's prisoners, Major Artur von Casimir, was charged with the assault. Brent had not seen who had hit him.

Later, building materials were made available to the men to rebuild and repair their barracks. As for shackling the men, this was finally abandoned in mid-December 1942.

Until late 1946 Kretschmer and the crew of U-99 stayed in Canada, but by this time, many prisoners were being sent back to the United Kingdom, and soon the turn came for them. They were brought back to Liverpool on board the SS *Aquitania*, then separated. The crew were sent to Camp 168 (or Camp 176) Glen Mill Camp at Oldham, in Lancashire, whereas Kretschmer and the officers were sent on to Camp 17, Lodge Moor Camp, near Sheffield. The crew members were fairly quickly repatriated but because U-boat commanders were seen as dangerous prisoners whose ideology remained intact, they were held longer in the more secure camps around the United Kingdom. Watten saw the arrival of forty U-boat captains with Kretschmer amongst them in early January 1947.

Two months later the U-boat ace was sent to a prisoner of war camp in Carmarthen in Wales. He was suffering from a stomach problem. During his time at Watten, Kretschmer had been interrogated along with the other U-boat captains held there but while he was recovering, the interrogator returned, baying for Kretschmer's blood over an incident in the north of England. A U-boat had been captured and it was assumed that he had sent a co-prisoner out of the camp to scuttle it. This aside, he had been involved in a mock court martial that had found the crew of the U-boat as cowards for allowing it to be taken by the enemy. Following further investigation, Kretschmer was told he would face a British court martial and that he would only return to Germany as one of the last prisoners of war in British hands. Just after this, he was sent to Camp 18, Featherstone Park near Haltwhistle, Northumberland and from here he was finally transferred to Germany to Neuengamme near Hamburg. After a hearing and a further wait, Kretschmer was released without charge.

A year later, Otto Wilhelm August Kretschmer married a doctor, Luise-Charlotte. In 1955, he joined the Bundesmarine, which was tiny in comparison to the navy he had joined in the 1930s. In 1957 he became commander of the 1 Geleitgeschwader, I Escot Squadron, and a year later became commander of the amphibian forces, the Amphibische Streitkräfte. He rose through the ranks until in 1965 he became Chief of Staff of the NATO Command for the Baltic Approaches. He stayed in this position for four years. During that time, he visited Orkney on several occasions in his NATO capacity and led an inquiry into the loss of the submarine *Hai*, which had been heading for Scotland on a goodwill gesture in September 1966. Nineteen lives were lost on a submarine that had been scuttled in 1945, salvaged and re-commissioned in the mid-1950s. Kretschmer noted many failings with the boat and the crew. He finally retired in 1970. His final rank was Flotillenadmiral, but even though he was no longer part of the German navy, he still held a keen interest in all things naval. In 1998 he died suddenly whilst on holiday in Bavaria at the age of 86.

In Orkney an obituary appeared for Kretschmer in *The Orcadian* newspaper on Thursday 19 November 1998 such had been his impact on the far north of Scotland.

Kretschmer's impact on the U-boat campaign can never be ignored. However, it is important to note that in the early stages of the U-boat war it was down to the commanding officers of each of the mismatched ships protecting the Allied convoys to take the initiative rather than any predetermined plan to protect the convoys. It was only later that the two groups hammered out plans and went on exercise. Thus, the U-boat war in the sea slowly petered out.

Chapter 11

Other Men of Note at Camp 165

Among the other men of note at Watten were SS-Oberführer Otto Baum, SS-Oberführer Walther Ewert and Kaptainleutnant Hans-Joachim von Morstein.

Otto Baum was born in Stetten-Hechingen on 15 November 1911. After leaving school, he went on to university to study agriculture. In 1935 he went to the Junkerschule in Brauschweig for final infantry training in April of that year. He became a platoon leader in 1936 in the II Battalion of the SS-Standarte Germania in Arolsen and was promoted to SS-Untersturmführer. In December the following year, having been at the army sports school in Wünsdorf, he was promoted once more to Obersturmführer. In 1938 he became Zugführer with 12 Kompanie of the Regiment Der Führer. By 1939 he had taken over control of 7 Kompanie of the Leibstandarte SS Adolf Hitler, and fought in the Polish campaign, where he received the Iron Cross 2nd Class. For his work in the western campaign with LSSAH, he received the Iron Cross 1st Class. The LSSAH met fierce resistance from the French but they overcame this and France fell into German hands. Following on from this Otto Baum took over the command of the III Battalion of the SS-Totenkopf division and saw action in the Russian campaign, breaking through the defences of the 34th Russian Army. In late December 1941, after a number of successes, he received the German Cross in Gold and the Knights Cross in May 1942. In November 1942 he was promoted once again, this time to SS-Obersturmbannführer in charge of the I Battalion of the SS Totenkopf infantry. In 1943 he took command of SS-Panzergrenadierregiment 5 Totenkopf and after fighting in the Third Battle of Kharkov, was awarded the Oak Leaves while he recovered from an injury sustained during the battle in Breslau. Once fully recovered, he returned and took over his post once more before being promoted yet again, this time to SS-Standartenführer. Following on from his experiences on the eastern front, he took lecture tours round the country and spoke of his experiences.

After the Normandy invasion, Baum was asked to take over the 17 SS-Panzergrenadierdivision *Götz von Berlichingen* as its divisional brigade leader had been seriously wounded in action. Baum ended up fighting at Falaise and retreated back to Metz, ensuring his troops a safe passage. For this, he received the Swords to add to the Oak Leaves, and was only the ninety-fifth person in the Wehrmacht to be awarded it. On 17 September 1944 Baum was finally promoted to SS-Oberführer.

By the end of January 1945, Baum and his men of the 16 SS-Panzergrenadierdivision found themselves pushed back to the River Po, and on 8 May 1945 he was captured and sent to an English prisoner of war camp before finally reaching Watten in 1947.

While at Camp 165, Baum was classed as a 'C+' political prisoner but after a short stay at the camp, Baum, D'Alquen and Wünsche were requested to be moved from Camp 165 as it was 'not suitable' for them and return to Featherstone Park at Haltwhistle, Northumberland. They were to be joined by another prisoner from Watten called Kummert. Otto Baum died in 1998.

SS-Oberführer Walther Ewert is recorded at being held in Watten in 1947 and had also been given the political grading of 'C+'. He had been born in November 1903 in the province of Prosen. He joined the army in 1921 and by 1935 had risen through the ranks. This year also saw him join the Nazi Party and the SS. He joined the Leibstandarte SS Adolf Hitler and was commissioned Obersturmführer on 20 April. Exactly ten years later he was promoted to Oberführer. Endorsed by 'Sepp' Dietrich, he was awarded the War Service Cross with Swords in December 1944 because he had managed to keep the supplies from reaching the troops under increasingly difficult circumstances, especially after the damage inflicted in Normandy in 1944 on the road and rail networks. Other medals he had received were the German Cross in Silver and the Iron Cross 2nd Class as well as the Reich's Sports Badge in Bronze. He remained with the LSSAH until the end of the war when the Americans captured him. He spent three years in captivity, leaving his wife and two children at home to wait for him. He died in 1976.

Kaptainleutnant Hans-Joachim von Morstein was as dangerous as his fellow compatriot Otto Kretschmer though his successes were on a much smaller scale. Von Morstein had been born in the city of Karlsruhe in the south-west of Germany near to the French-German border in August 1909. By December 1943 he had been educated and trained up to the rank of U-boat Kaptainleutnant, taking over U-483 on 22 December that year and remaining in that position until 8 May 1945. In late August 1944, U-483 left Kiel in Schleswig-Holstein in northern Germany en route to Horten in Norway where she arrived two days later. From there, the U-boat sailed on to Stavanger where she stayed until she set sail again, this time en route to Bergen, spending seven weeks at sea patrolling British waters. It was during this time she had her only triumph. The British frigate HMS *Whitaker* was severely damaged on 1 November off the coast of Eire. U-483's final tour of duty took her from Bergen to Trondheim, where she arrived on 26 March 1945.

In December 1944 Hans-Joachim von Morstein was awarded the German Cross in Gold for the sinking of HMS *Whitaker*. He was captured as a prisoner of war and spent time at Camp 184 at Llanmartin in Wales before spending time at Camp 165 in Watten. After screening at the camp, he was given the political grading of 'B-'.

In 1948 HMS *Whitaker* was broken up. U-483 was transferred from Trondheim in Norway to Scapa Flow in the Orkney Islands before being sent on to Loch Ryan on the west coast of Scotland, at the head of which lies the town of Stranraer. It sank on 16 December 1945, although it is not clear if it was scuttled like the other captured U-boats in the loch.

Untersturmführer Erich Zepper was also held at Camp 165. He had been born at Sebnitz in Saxony very close to the Swiss border in November 1915. He was assigned to the 2 SS-Panzergrenadierregiment *Westland* and 5 SS-Panzerdivision *Wiking*. He fought on the Eastern Front and was awarded the EK1 Infantry Assault Badge, the Wound Badge, and the Ritterkreuz, or Knight's Cross, was awarded to him in December 1943. The British held him until 1948.

Karl Weschke, the famous artist, was also incarcerated at Watten for a time. Born near Gera in the province of Thuringen on 7 June 1925, Weschke was abandoned at the age of two by his mother who placed him in a children's home, although she did come back for him five years later. He became a member of the Hitler Youth where the military regime suited him as it gave him the stability he had never had as a young child. He left school at the age of fourteen and went on to join the Luftwaffe in 1942 but during a short stint in the Low Countries he was captured and sent firstly to Chepstow, but after an altercation with an interrogation officer, he was sent to Watten. Here he learned that his father, whom he had only met once when he was a child, had died in a concentration camp and it was this news that made him decide to become a British citizen. It was also at Watten, through the encouragement of one of the chaplains, that he took to carving: then painting followed naturally to him. From Watten, he was sent to England and after he was released from captivity in the spring of 1948, he worked in Scotland for a time for the Ministry of Agriculture and Forestry. He married Alison, his first wife, in 1948. They finally settled in Cornwall in 1955 but two years later the couple divorced. The choice of Cornwall was mainly due to the influence and friendship formed with the artist Bryan Winter. It was in Cornwall where he became well known for his modern pieces of art. Much of his art was dark in mood. He painted abstract landscapes and included bodies floating in the seas and dogs bearing their teeth viciously. Later, influenced by trips to Egypt, the paintings showed the loneliness, solitude and vulnerability so common in his other works. In the 1990s the Tate Gallery in London acquired some of his paintings and back in Germany he was finally recognised for his works and his contribution to modern art by being given honorary citizenship of Gera. Among his most famous works are *Fighting Dogs 1978* and *The Fire-Eater with Spectators 1984–86*. He became firm friends with the author John le Carré who wrote about him after his death in February 2005. Weschke married three times and had five children.

Chapter 12

The London District Cage

The London District Cage was the main interrogation centre in the United Kingdom. Myths and half-truths have been in evidence since its inception simply because the work carried out there was top secret. At the helm was Lt.-Col. Alexander Paterson Scotland, a one-time soldier in the German army during its time in South-West Africa in the early twentieth century. He had left his native Scotland, following in the footsteps of his brother, and worked initially for South African Territories Ltd, a grocery company which supplied the German army near Cape Town. On two separate occasions, he was told to learn all about the German army so he would one day 'be a valuable man to your country', and later, by the Germans themselves, was told to learn German fluently and there would be opportunities for him. By 1915 Scotland had returned to Great Britain and sought intelligence work in Whitehall. His work took him to France, Belgium and Holland after being accepted into the Inns of Court Officers' Training Corps and he began his career, interrogating German prisoners of war in their own language.

During the 1920s Scotland and his wife went to South America due to his new job with a commercial enterprise, where he made discreet enquiries about the German communities there. It surprised him how large it was becoming in Argentina. However, in 1933 the couple returned to England.

By the eve of the outbreak of World War II, Scotland had been given an insight into the Third Reich. On several occasions he had made the trip to Germany and noted the changes for himself. On a visit to a Captain Schmidt in Stuttgart, Scotland was amazed to see that on his desk was a file labelled 'Schottland'. They had profiled him. That aside, he had meetings with the Minister of Agriculture and watched the rallies at Nuremburg as the people poured adoration on their leader. He became aware of the ruthlessness of the Gestapo, the state secret police, and the growing hatred for the Jewish population. What angered him most was when he discovered that both in South America and Europe there was talk of dealing with the Jewish Question and anti-Nazis with the building of penal camps.

On one occasion, in the late 1930s, Scotland visited an old friend near Munich. They had known each other since their South African days and Scotland was intrigued as to why his friend was so keen to hear his stories on South Africa. A day later, he was invited to tea and introduced to another guest – Adolf Hitler. Hitler questioned Scotland about South America and moved on to South West Africa, which he declared should be returned to German control. Scotland found him direct, almost amusing at times, but his host seemed nervous throughout the meeting and, when Hitler left, advised Scotland to never speak of the conference and certainly not to report it to anyone as it was highly confidential.

In March 1939, at a restaurant, Scotland sat with some executives and listened to their talk for fifteen minutes before speaking. He listened to them talking of Hitler's Germany and agreeing with his tactics in dealing with Jews, not to mention that war would not break out. Scotland retorted. He spoke of his time in Germany, of Himmler's SS men and the Gestapo, and of young boys parading the streets with weapons. Many in the company were astonished and questioned him more on the German situation, which he duly obliged. He told them it was not a question of 'if' war would break out, but 'when?'.

At the age of sixty, the War Office asked Scotland to help in the field of intelligence and asked him to set up, at suitable sites across the United Kingdom, prisoner of war cages where interrogations would take place. At these cages, prisoners of war were to be interrogated before being sent on to prisoner of war camps. Many different places were used for the cages, such as the racecourse at Doncaster. These courses had all the open space required and good accommodation. In one incident, as Scotland dealt with the organisation of the cages, he was informed of a strike at one of the camps. Out of 3000 prisoners, 500 were refusing to work or draw their rations. If left, the situation could have worsened, but Scotland visited the camp, addressed the men in their native tongue and managed to persuade the bulk of them that their protest was futile. Prisoners could not be allowed to dictate how a camp was run. Eventually, as the war came to a close, the war crimes interrogation headquarters in Kensington Palace Gardens in London, which became known simply as the London District Cage, was set up. Aiding Scotland in his role was Major A. F. A. I. Terry, who was in charge of all the interrogations at the London District Cage. Joining them was Captain A. Ryder and Lt P. A. Hepton who both acted as interrogators along with assistant interrogators Captain E. Egger and Captain C. C. Hay.

Numbers 6–8 Kensington Palace Gardens are houses in the grand style. But during the 1940s these houses were taken over by the War Crimes Investigation Unit, to deal with the more serious war crimes committed by prisoners of war in British hands. Over a period of time, a huge amount of documents and statements were gathered from the prisoners. Along with material given over to the Cage by MI19, these documents formed the basis of the interrogations that took place. Between October 1945 and September 1948, around 3500 prisoners of war and enemy civilians passed through the Cage. Over a thousand statements were taken. A number of prominent cases were passed to the courts, such as those involving the Devizes plot, when Rosterg was murdered at Cultybraggan, and Fritz Knöchlein, who was involved in mass murders at Paradis in 1940 when he ordered the execution of one hundred and twenty-four British soldiers at Dunkirk, many from the Royal Norfolk Regiment. Soldiers from this regiment knew they had been beaten by the Germans and had approached with the white flag of surrender but it was ignored. They tried again after this first group had been fired upon. It was ignored once more. In a very short space of time, over one hundred men lay in the meadow at Paradis dead and dying from machine-gun fire on the orders of Fritz Knöchlein. Knöchlein's trial took place in Hamburg in October 1948 and he was sentenced to death. He was executed early in 1949. The most famous case to be dealt with however was Sagan, also known as Stalag Luft III, when, in 1943, fifty Allied airmen were deliberately shot when they were recaptured after escaping from their prison camp. After collecting as much data as they could, at a court in Hamburg in September 1947, eighteen of the men involved in the executions were brought to trial. Fourteen were sentenced to death, although one had his sentence commuted to life imprisonment. Two others were sentenced to life imprisonment and the last two were sentenced to ten years. Scotland was later to write that Sagan and its story 'should not be forgotten'.

Later, in a copy of a conversation in January 1945, Scotland came into the possession of notes regarding the movement of the allied prisoners still held at Stalg Luft III, in which Goering said that the 10,000 air force men should be left to 'their Soviet Russian allies' or, if they were to be transported, they should do so 'with their pants and boots off so they cannot run away in the snow'. Hitler ordered that they had to be taken out of the camp by 'every possible means'. This was the kind of evidence used at the trials of the prisoners of war in British hands who had committed war crimes.

The London District Cage also dealt with the incident at Wormhoudt with the execution of the British soldiers there, as well as those crimes related to the concentration camps, including Stutthof. The Cage also dealt with applications for passports so prisoners could move on to different countries and with problems arising from the prisoners having too close contact with the local communities in which they were held.

Certain rules were laid down. Firstly, the crime had to be identified as being a truly wilful criminal act which would justify a length sentence or death to the perpetrator. Witnesses were to be sought in order make statements against the accused which would stand up in court. Interrogators would work hand in hand with interpreters who would cover many different languages, and all statements were translated into English and the accused's native tongue. The legal department was set up to sift though all the evidence, decide on who were to be witnesses and prepared the case for trial. One of the main concerns was security. A secure building to hold the prisoners was of paramount importance, but it had to have segregated areas and at least four rooms that could be used on a daily basis to be used during interrogation. Scotland was in a unique position for he knew the German language, the German manner and German customs, which many at the Cage did not. This was their opportunity to learn. During the course of the interrogations, the officers were able to learn about the German character, the German way of life and further their language skills. It was only by their work at the Cage they could get such insight into the men. It was noted that if a future war included the United Kingdom, 'a unit to cover the higher grade of interrogation … must be established'.

One of the roles of the Cage was to work with the British Security Services, but all the interrogations done at the LDC were to be under strict military conditions. This was seen as the best way of achieving results. The statements were passed between the two organisations so a case could be formed against those who were alleged war criminals. Each statement was given a code, such as PWIS(H)/LDC/... for the London Cage interrogations and KP or LF for the other two interrogation centres at Kempton Park and Lingfield. PWIS stood for prisoner of war Interrogation Section.

The methods used at the Cage for interrogation are still wrapped in myths and half-truths. Scotland himself used different methods. In one case, when a young man was brought in for interrogation, Scotland and the man giggled for part of the interview. The boy had been one of only a handful of survivors from the German warship *Bismarck* and simply due to nerves could not stop giggling when asked a question no matter how mundane it was. Scotland laughed with him, posed questions about his family and home and finally asked for military information, which eventually he succeeded in attaining. Other methods included writing down their side of the story. Sometimes prisoners would be part of the same event but they told different versions in front of their comrades. In order to establish the truth, Scotland asked them to go into a room and write down what they could remember. Scotland had reiterated this to the men serving under him. He believed the only way to get these prisoners into court was by setting them aside and leaving them to write their own statement in complete isolation so that when it arrived at court there could be no denials when their day in court came. In this way, some would sign their own death warrants.

After the written statements were completed, or the interrogation was comprehensively exhausted, notes were made and a final report written. The report would begin with a preamble of when and where the interview took place, the name of the prisoner and from which camp he had been sent, then it would highlight the prisoner's history with much more detail in the section when he had joined the forces. The report would end with a conclusion on the merits or otherwise of the prisoner being put forward for further investigation or trial.

Occasionally, however, things got out of hand at the Cage. In one instance, a German naval officer in full uniform was seen on his hands and knees, scrubbing the floor. In others, prisoners were forced to kneel for a great length of time, while they were beaten around the head. Sleep deprivation is an age-old tactic and this too took place in Kensington as a form of torture. Scotland himself was asked by a defence counsel in the case of Erich Zacharias if he had threatened torture using electrical devices, had been refused food and deprived of sleep as well as pulled him by the hair across the floor. Scotland wholly refuted the allegations, and demonstrated the hair pulling in the court using a volunteer, but it was at this time the British newspapers heard he had been in the German army and all kinds of accusations were published. Headlines included 'MI5 Colonel on Nazi general Staff' and 'Britain's Master Spy'. Scotland rode the storm. He was at pains to point out that MI5 was at that time highly romanticised and that at no point did he personally work for the organisation, which was part of the War Office and dealt with the armed forces. He was an official of the War Office's legal branch.

Some of the questions asked at the Cage included: 'Do you think the Nazis system was a good idea?' and 'Were you a member of the Nazi Party and if so when did you join?'. They were asked about work they had done both under the Weimar Government and under Hitler's Reich and about family life. Those who had worked in certain areas of Germany were asked to draw sketches of their barracks and give details of ranks and numbers of men. Their full military history was asked for and many of those interrogated at the Cage gave details of incidents such as bullying, beatings and shootings of the ordinary soldiers if they failed to do their duty in accordance with what was expected of them by their superiors.

In 1950 Scotland had completed the first draft of his memoirs and sent it to the War Office in order that it could be censored if necessary. The War Office was furious with some of Scotland's admission as to what went on at the Cage, including breaches of the Geneva Convention 1925, and he was allegedly threatened under the Official Secrets Act unless he withdrew the book.

In 1957 a new edited version of the book was finally published under the title 'The London Cage'. By this time Scotland had been awarded the Order of the British Empire for his work at the interrogation unit. In 2006 the file containing his manuscripts, which had been held at the National Archives in Kew under the Official Secrets Act 1911, was finally opened to the public.

The full extent of what happened at the London District Cage and the other two main interrogation centres may never be fully known. What is known is that men from the prisoner of war camp 165 were interrogated there for their part in the Nazi regime along with many hundreds more. Between October 1945 and September 1948, 3573 prisoners of war and enemy civilians passed through the Cage, many of whom were brought to Kensington to provide more information on war crimes. Over 1000 statements were taken and presented at the war crimes tribunals, including that taking place at Nuremberg.

Chapter 13

The Polish Contingent

The history of the camp at Watten would not be complete without a mention of the Polish troops who were in Caithness at that time. Since the fifteenth century, Scotland had strong links with Poland. The two countries had traded food, coal, timber and cattle and each country had developed blood ties. Over the centuries, Poland had been swinging between having its own monarchy and being independent to being occupied by its neighbours. Only twenty years before the outbreak of World War II, she had become independent under the Treaty of Versailles. When Poland was invaded in 1939, the links between Scotland, indeed the United Kingdom, became even stronger.

The first wave of Polish refugees arrived in 1940 in just the clothes they stood up in, but because they were so anti-German, they were warmly welcomed. Initially, they lived in camps but over time built wooden huts. In June 1940 the Polish Government in Exile in London signed an agreement whereby a Polish army and air force were formed and helped Britain to defend not only her shores but also saw action on the Continent. It was thought that Germany would mount an invasion from Norway along the Fife and Angus coastline, so many of the Polish soldiers were stationed in these areas, building defences right along the coast. The men of military age were formed into units and were based all over the country from Kelso in the Borders to Wick. At their height, there were over 75,000 Polish troops in Scotland. Many saw fighting in north-western Europe. The 1st Polish Armoured Division, which had been formed in Scotland, landed in France in August 1944 and joined the Canadians, helping to close the Falaise gap. The Polish Navy took part in the Normandy landings, having been deployed on numerous occasions in helping the British, including escorting the Atlantic convoys. Its merchant shipping also helped with keeping vital supply routes open. As for the Polish Air Force, they helped Britain to defend her shores during the Battle of Britain in 1940, shot down almost two hundred V1 bombs, and dropped aid to the resistance forces in occupied Europe.

In Poland itself an underground movement had been formed. The Home Army made life as difficult as possible for the German occupying forces by gathering intelligence and using sabotage tactics against the military and industrial plants taken over by them. In 1944 this accumulated in the Warsaw uprising which lasted over sixty days but was eventually crushed decisively. Heinrich Himmler gave orders for the city to be razed to the ground and its inhabitants shot. The Wehrmacht destroyed over 90% of the city and over 500,000 of its inhabitants were sent to concentration camps. Almost 250,000 died in the fighting. Those found guilty of taking part were either given long prison sentences or executed.

Throughout the war, Polish intelligence helped the Allies by gathering information on troop movements in Europe, as well as details of aircraft deployments and naval objectives. Two of their greatest achievements were discovering the plans for Barbarossa in June 1941 and the information they had gathered on Enigma, which they handed over to the British authorities. Poland got its hands on its first Enigma machine in 1928 by chance, and by 1929, had organised a group of mathematicians to break the code. By 1933 Poland was reading the Enigma traffic. Only days before the outbreak of war, the authorities handed over their own manufactured machines and the codes to the British. This guaranteed the British would help them in their hour of need. One of the major inventions made by Polish technicians, and used by the British Army, was a mine detector. This proved to be invaluable. Thus Poland played a vital part in the Allied war effort.

When the war ended Poland remained under Soviet influence and many of the Polish troops stationed in Scotland were reluctant to return home to a communist state – but the puppet Polish Government needed them to return to help with reconstruction. It did not help that Germany had proved that the Soviet invaders in Poland had murdered some 4000 Polish officers at Katyn Forest near Smolensk in Russia when the mass grave was discovered there in 1943. This atrocity was admitted to by Soviet President Mikhail Gorbachev only in 1990 when he expressed 'profound regret' for the massacre by the NKVD, the Soviet security force. The other problem was, of course, that Poland had lost land and some of the Polish people had no homes to go back to as they no longer existed as part of Poland under the terms thrashed out at Yalta in 1945. Poland lost almost half her land and although Stalin had promised free elections at Yalta, these failed to materialise. It was also at Yalta that the Allies withdrew their recognition of the Polish Government in Exile which was a bitter blow to those still stationed in Scotland.

In Britain there was a growing perception that the Polish people were taking jobs away from the returning troops who had been demobbed. The United Kingdom had a major problem on its hands which was borne out at Skitten.

The Polish soldiers had a profound impact on the county. Many of them were housed at Skitten, a few miles from Wick on the Castletown road. Much of their accommodation is still in existence, now used for agricultural purposes. Made from concrete, the long buildings are intermittently broken up by barred windows with roofs that are still in fairly good condition considering they are over sixty years old. The small number of these buildings *in situ* gives an idea of what the camp at Skitten looked like. However, unlike the Germans held at Watten, the Poles, some of whom were in fact German nationals, were not treated quite so well. Many local people at the time were suspicious of the Polish soldiers especially after incidents in Castletown, and in their dealings with rationing. The first real problems arose in March 1947.

At the camp at Skitten, known as No. 1 Polish Recalcitrants Camp, five hundred Polish soldiers went on hunger strike, partly because of being labelled 'recalcitrants' but also because of the Polish Resettlement Corps. The Corps had been set up in 1946 to deal with the Polish question of repatriation but worse from the Polish point of view was that it put an end to hopes that the Soviet Union would leave their homeland and to return home meant going to a communist country under the dictatorship of Josef Stalin. The Corps intended to help the now former troops to find work but much of this was well below the skills of the men. However, in Caithness, it was possible for them to go into agriculture or forestry, but what they really wanted was to be able to emigrate. Perhaps it did not help their reputation having the label of being disobedient and unmanageable in their relations with the people of the county. Everyone knew of the camp and its title, therefore they believed everyone inside must have been problematic, yet it was not the case. Of course, with five hundred men there, there would inevitably be some that would cause trouble, but it was just a minority group that gave the Poles such a bad name. Lt.-Col. A. T. B. Bignold de Cologan, the camp's commandant, had already spoken to the men of the Government's programme for resettlement. He claimed they were being offered certain advantages such as employment in civilian jobs within the United Kingdom, the chance of bringing their families over, or emigration. The only concession the Polish soldiers had to make was to join the Polish Resettlement Corps. Bignold de Cologan had met some delegates from the camp to explain these opportunities but the men were deeply unhappy. On the morning of 4 March three black flags were hoisted above the huts near the camp's main gates. A seven-foot square board was placed at the camp entrance with a proclamation, written in black and red, announcing:

> Here are no recalcitrants. Here are no undecided. Here are all Polish soldiers from Africa and Italy, soldiers decided for emigration. We insist upon removal of Polish officers from here and admission of correspondents; a demobilisation in Great Britain; a free emigration without joining the Polish Resettlement Corps. We are protesting against calling us recalcitrant and undecided, against deportation to Germany, and as the sign of protestation, we have begun a hunger strike from March 4th, hour 10 a.m.

Some of the Poles wanted nothing more than to emigrate to the United States or Canada but they did not want to join the PRC in order to do so as they saw it as contrary to the Polish constitution. None of them wanted to return to Germany as they believed their reception there would not be good. It was clear from their notice that the ordinary conscripts did not trust, nor indeed like, the Polish officers who were with them.

A day later, as blizzards struck Caithness, the men continued their strike. Not only that but the camp cooks joined them. None of the men had eaten anything since breakfast on the 4th. As the news spread of the hunger strike, the local Member of Parliament for Caithness and Sutherland, Mr E. L. Gander Dower, undertook a pledge to raise the issue of the use of the word 'recalcitrant' in the House of Commons; it seemed to him it was only given to certain units within the Polish forces and was therefore unfair.

Voluntarily staying in the camp, the strike continued into a third day. Many of the men however were beginning to feel the effects of not eating for such a long period of time and were confined to their huts. The poor wintry weather continued. It was reported locally that no one, on this third day, was picketing at the board by the camp entrance. During the early afternoon, the decision was taken to abandon the strike. A delegation of men met with Lt.-Col. Bignold de Cologan once more and informed him the strike would end at 4 p.m. The men were in a poor way. Many were so weak they were taken to the local hospital in Wick for treatment. The camp commandant arranged for light meals to be prepared for the hunger strikers and this was to continue until the men had regained their health. What stunned Bignold de Cologan was the fact the other three Polish camps he was in charge of did not follow the actions of the men at Skitten. Why they did not follow suit is unclear. However, the Poles in Castletown caused a furore that planted the seed of distrust among the local population a few days later and it was one that was to grow as the incidents mounted.

A week after the end of the Skitten strike, at the Rifle Hall in Wick, where a dance had been taking place, a number of Polish recalcitrants were involved in a knifing incident. This was the second such incident involving knives. The other had occurred in Castletown on Wednesday night, just the day before, where the Polish troops had been fighting outside the Drill Hall in the town. On that occasion, a Polish military policeman was stabbed and stones were thrown between the British troops sent there to help the Polish military police and the recalcitrants. Now, soldiers from the Watten prisoner of war camp were once again helping in Wick. All of the Polish soldiers involved were transported back to their camp at Castletown and the British soldiers went with them. Around one hundred and fifty men from Watten paraded the streets of the town, clearly displaying their arms.

An inquiry into the stabbing of the military policeman began on Saturday 15 March, with the Poles being paraded past the injured man. He managed to identify from his ambulance bed several of those involved and eight of them from a total of fifty-two picked out ended up in the police cells in Wick in connection with the stabbing. These incidents were very much an eye-opener for not only the local population by also the military. At a meeting of the Caithness County Council Administration and Finance Committee in Wick on 24 April, it was decided to write to the Secretary of State for Scotland and the Scottish Command headquarters to set out their concerns about the Polish units and their behaviour. Not only was blame laid firmly on them for the disturbances, as pointed out very powerfully by Provost Brims in Thurso, but other committee members also spoke of the increase in house break-ins in the local areas of Thurso and Castletown. Overall, they agreed that the Poles behaviour was out of control and something had to be done. The people of Caithness, it was suggested, needed to be protected. The Polish Military Police, they concluded, were not able to deal with the men alone and they decided that the men should be treated like the British soldiers who had to be back in barracks by a certain hour.

A month later, Councillor J. Abrach Mackay, at a meeting of the Caithness Police Committee, pleaded for more of a police presence in Castletown and claimed that the Poles were under no military discipline whatsoever. One policeman in Castletown, Mr John Mackay, said he was woefully inadequate especially under the circumstances. The Poles were, in his own words, 'without heart, without work, without hope. They are stricken with moral death'. He went on to complain that the Government had not done enough to help them.

However, the Chief Constable, W. K. Cormack, told him an order would be through within a few days under which the men would be subject to British military discipline and three more recruits were in place as well as frequent patrols by a police car to clamp down on indiscipline.

But the final straw for most Caithnessians came in the form of food parcels. They found out the Polish soldiers were sending gift parcels back home to relatives in Poland and elsewhere in Europe. Although gift parcels, albeit with strict permission only, could be sent abroad, it was a stipulation that the men sacrificed part of their own rations and the packages had to be declared at the local food office in Wick. Yet, the Caithness Food Control Committee found the men were able to buy up to 3 lb of tea, costing 6s. 6d. per pound, and sugar at 1s. 6d. a pound, but they could not fathom out where the men were getting these rationed supplies from. After an investigation, Mr William Mackenzie of Castletown told the Committee the Poles were selling what was termed 'suit lengths' of materials. He himself had been offered some beautiful material for just such a deal. It was only having given the matter much thought, he believed that while men were on leave in the south, they were able to buy food and materials and brought them back to Caithness to sell on the black market. Mr Anderson, the food executive officer, said that he had received other complaints about the sending of food parcels abroad and had taken up the matter with his Divisional Food Office. The Office informed him they had been inundated with complaints from all over Caithness where the Poles were stationed. He believed the matter was well in hand and there was absolutely no black marketeering in the county. However, the local MP, Mr Gander Dower, had been overwhelmed by the number of local constituents complaining to him regarding the parcels. He asked for an investigation into the matter as the allegations were serious, especially those made against the men stationed at Skitten and Castletown. In a letter to the Food Minister, he said the Poles were sending away many substantial parcels containing tea, sugar and various other goods from the rationing points system, and the number of these had grown substantially. Yet he was not prepared to raise the issue in the House of Commons. This was because of the already entrenched ill-feeling in the county but he believed that the sending of these parcels was illegal and deprived some people of their food rations. A Mr Strachey was appointed investigator.

It was at this time the long awaited British troops arrived from the south to deal with the indiscipline amongst the Poles. In mid-August 1947 it was announced by the Scottish Command that a company of British troops would be sent to Caithness in order to boost morale and deal with the constant indiscipline. The men were to be stationed in Thurso in huts at the east end of the transit camp which had been closed down by the military the previous December. The time the Polish troops had left in Caithness was running out fast. The Gordon Highlanders arrived from Edinburgh in late August. They were assigned to demonstrate to the Poles how disciplined they were and set an example to them. There were only three hundred Polish troops left in the county by this time and all of them were now stationed in either Castletown or Skitten. On 24 November the last contingent of Poles left by special train from Thurso. There were only one hundred men on board, with between 2000 and 3000 already finding their way back to Europe.

It was due mainly to their indiscipline and dealings with the rations towards the end of their stay in the far north that set them against some of the local population. They had been the first foreigners to stay in Caithness, and in particular in the camp at Watten. However, many eventually settled in Scotland and today there are Polish groups still in the country who are proud of their role in World War II and their fight against Nazism and communism.

In 1990 Poland regained her independence once more.

Chapter 14

Conclusion

The history of Camp 165 in Watten should not be ignored or forgotten. It is just as important as the histories of other camps such as Camp 21 at Comrie or Stalag Luft III. Many of the men held at Watten were regular soldiers who had been conscripted and had fought in a war in which they had no choice. Others, such as d'Alquen, Wünsche and Hoppe, may be famous in their own right for the part they played in the regime but they too had been caught up by the promises made by Adolf Hitler about a greater Germany. Watten today can sit proud in the knowledge that it played a vital role both during and in the aftermath of World War II, and hopefully this book dispels some myths which have sprung up around the camp.

Many believe that World War II was a completely separate conflict from World War I, yet studies bear out that it was simply a continuation. Germany had already been viewed as an aggressive country long before the outbreak of war in 1914 because of her annexation tendencies. The German people did not have what the Americans call 'closure' after World War I and, by eroding the treaties signed in 1919 at the Paris Peace Settlement, and rearmament taking place in defiance of international disapproval, the 1920s and 1930s saw Germany rise once more to dominate Europe. It had begun in Hitler's own writings in *Mein Kampf.* In that book he declared Germany's need for *Lebensraum* attached to the 'Motherland' and it is clear that Germany, in his opinion, had to turn towards the lands of the East. By 1933 Hitler was proclaimed Chancellor. Once in power, he slowly began Germany's ascendancy. He withdrew the country from the League of Nations. In 1934 he became Führer and a year later had established the Luftwaffe, which had been forbidden under the terms of Versailles. In 1936 Germany troops occupied the Rhineland and two years later she forcibly annexed Austria. Czechoslovakia was forced to cede the Sudetenland to Germany and six months later in March 1939, Czechoslovakia was broken up. It had been a war of diplomatic attrition during all that time. It only spilled over to a 'hot war' of serious fighting following her invasion of Poland in 1939. Again, this stemmed from the terms of Versailles, as she had lost the

Polish Corridor, Upper Silesia and West Prussia as punishment for causing World War I. As far as Germany was concerned, she was only taking back what was rightfully hers.

All over Europe, thousands of soldiers, sailors and airmen were taken prisoner by enemy forces during the fighting during World War II. Some were never to return home. But of those who did, each one had a story to tell. Some have spoken of the harsh treatments they received at the hands of their captors whilst others have spoken of how it changed their lives in a positive way. Many who were held at Watten seem to have left with positive memories of their treatment. They certainly held Lt.-Col. Murray in high regard. Their acceptance by the local population has also been evident throughout this researched work. Caithnessians won the hearts and minds of many of the captives.

Bibliography and Sources

Abarinov, V. (1993) *The Murders of Katyn,* Hippocrene Books.

Ailsbury, C. (1998) *SS: Hell on the Eastern Front*, Spellmount Publishers.

Argyle, C. (1980) *Chronology of World War II*, Marshall Cavendish.

Bell, P. M. H. (1997) *The Origins of the Second World War*, second edition, Longman.

Bessel, R. (1993) *Germany after the First World War*, Clarendon Press.

Bishop, C. (2003) *SS: Hell on the Western Front*, Spellmount Publishers.

Bishop, C. (2004) *The Rise of Hitler's Third Reich*, Spellmount Publishers.

Boyce, R. *et al.* (2004) *The Origins of World War Two: The Debate Continues*, Palgrave Macmillan.

Burrin, P. (2005) *Nazi Anti-Semitism: From Prejudice to the Holocaust*, The New Press.

Carroll, T. (2005) *The Great Escape from Stalag Luft III: The Full Story of How 76 Allied Officers Carried Out World War II's Most Remarkable Mass Escape*, Pocket Books.

Clark, A. (2001) *Barbarossa: The Russian German Conflict*, Cassell.

D'Alquen, G. (1939) *Die SS Geschichte, Aufgabe und Organisation der Schutzstaffeln der NSDAP,* Junker and Dünnhaupt Verlag.

Davidson, E. (2001) *Chronology of World War Two*, Weidenfeld Military.

Davies, N. (2004) *Rising '44: The Battle for Warsaw*, Pan Books.

Doherty, R. (2004) *Normandy 1944: The Road to Victory*, Spellmount Publishers.

Erickson, J. (2003) *The Road to Berlin: Stalin's War with Germany*, Cassell.

Evans, R. J. (2003) *The Coming of the Third Reich*, Allen Lane.

Evans, R. J. (2006) *The Third Reich in Power*, Penguin Books.

Ford, K. (2003) *Juno Beach*, Sutton Publishing.

Gallately, R. (2003) *The Spectator of Genocide: Mass Murder in a Historical Perspective*, Cambridge University Press.

Gilbert, M. (2002) *The Second World War*, Weidenfeld.

Glantz, D. M. (2001) *Barbarossa: Hitler's Invasion of Russia, 1941*, NPI Media Group.

Glantz, D. M. (1998) *Kharkov: Anatomy of a Military Disaster*, Ian Allan Publishing.

Golby, J. *et al.* (2001) *Between Two Wars*, The Open University Press.

Goldstein, E. (2002) *The First World War Peace Settlements: From Versailles to Locarno 1919–25*, Longman.

Graf, J. *et al.* (1999) *Das Konzentrationslager Stutthof und seine Funktion in der nationalsozialistischen Judenpolitik*, Castle Hill Publishers.

Grant, R. G. (2006) *Barbarossa: The German Campaign in Russia – Planning and Operations*, Trafford Publishing.

Hastings, M. (2004) *Armageddon*, Macmillan.

Haining, P. (2002) *The Flying Bomb War: Contemporary Eyewitness Accounts of the German V1 and V2 Raids on Britain 1942–1945*, Robson Books.

Hargreaves, R. (2006) *The Germans in Normandy*, Pen and Sword Military.

Hitler, A. (1941) *Mein Kampf*, Franz Eher.

Hohne, H. *et al.* (2000) *The Order of the Death's Head: The Story of Hitler's SS*, Penguin Books.

Holbrooke, R. *et al.* (2002) *Paris 1919: Six Months that Changed the World*, Random House.

Jordan, D. (2004) *The Fall of Hitler's Third Reich*, Spellmount Publishers.

Keegan, J. (1997) *The Battle for History: Re-fighting World War Two*, Pimlico.

Kershaw, I. (1998) *Hitler: Hubris*, Allen Lane.

Kershaw, I. (2001) *Hitler: Nemesis*, Allen Lane.

Knopp, G. (2004) *Hitler's Holocaust*, Sutton Publishing.

Knopp, G. (2004) *The SS: A Warning from History*, Sutton Publishing.

Latawski, P. (2004) *Falaise Pocket*, Sutton Publishing.

Le Carre, J *et al.* (2005) *Karl Weschke 1925–2005*, Petronilla Silver.

Macintyre, D. (2004) *U-boat Killer*, Rigel Publications.

Maclean, F. (1998) *Camp Men: SS Officers Who Ran the Nazi Concentration Camp System*, Schiffer Publishing.

Meyer, H. (1994; 2005) *The History of the 12 SS-Panzerdivision 'Hitlerjugend'*, Stackpole Books.

McCosh, F. (1997) *Nissen of the Huts*, B D Publishing.

Neufeld, M. (1994) *The Rocket and the Reich: Peenemunde and the Coming of the Ballistic Missile Era*, Simon & Schuster.

Ogley, B. (1992) *Doodlebugs and Rockets: Battle of the Flying Bombs*, Froglets Publications.

Overy, R. (2004) *The Dictators*, Allen Lane.

Overy, R. (1997) *Russia's War*, Penguin Books.

Overy, R. J. (1998) *The Origins of the Second World War*, Longman.

Patten, M. (2004) *The War-Time Kitchen: Nostalgic Food and Facts from 1940–1954*, Hamlyn.

Piszkiewicz, D. (1995) *The Nazi Rocketeers: Dreams of Space and Crimes of War*, Greenwood Press.

Prien, G. (2004) *U-boat Commander*, Ceberus.

Purdue, A. W. (1999) *The Second World War*, Palgrave Macmillan.

Rees, L. (2005) *Auschwitz: The Nazis and the Final Solution*, BBC Books.

Rees, L. (1997) *The Nazis: A Warning from History*, BBC Books.

Ripley, T. (2001) *Steel Rain*, Motorbooks International.

Roberts, J. M. (1967; 2001) *Europe 1880–1945*, Longman.

Robertson, T. (1955; 2003) *The Golden Horseshoe*, Greenhill Books.

Ross, S. (2001) *Rationing*, Evan Brothers.

Scotland, A. P. (1957; 1973) *The London Cage*, George Mann.

Snydor, L. L. (1976) *Encyclopaedia of the Third Reich*, McGraw-Hill.

Syndor, C. W. (1992) *Soldiers of Destruction: The SS Death's Head Division 1933–1945*, Princeton University Press.

Taylor, A. J. P. (1991) *The Origins of the Second World War*, Penguin Books.

Taylor, B. (2003) *Barbarossa to Berlin: A Chronology of the Campaigns on the Eastern Front 1941–45 Long Drive East 22 June 1941 to 18 November 1942*, Spellmount Publishers.

Taylor, B. (2004) *Barbarossa to Berlin: A Chronology of the Campaigns on the Eastern Front 1941-45 November 1942 to May 1945*, Spellmount Publishers.

Waites, B, *et al.* (2001) *The Impact of World War* I, The Open University Press.

Williams, A. (2004) *D-Day to Berlin*, Hodder & Stoughton.

Williamson, G. (2005) *SS: Hitler's Instrument of Terror*, Motorbooks International.

Williamson, G. (2003) *Waffen-SS Handbook 1933–1945*, Sutton Publishing.

Williamson, G. (2005) *Wolf Pack: The Story of the U-boat in World War II*, Osprey.

Winchester, C. (2000) *Ostfront: Hitler's War on Russia 1941–45*, Osprey.

Wistrich, R.S. (1982) *Who's Who in Nazi Germany*, Routledge.

Zweiniger-Bargielowska, I. (2002) *Austerity in Britain: Rationing, Controls and Consumption, 1939–1955*, Oxford University Press.

National Archive Documents

FO 939/199

FO939/458

ADM199/2524

WO208/4294

WO311/689

Selected Websites

www.islandfarm.fsnet.co.uk

www.online-archaeology.co.uk

www.english-heritage.org.uk

stutthof.pl

uboat.net

www.caithness.org

www.subbrit.org.uk

www.wartimememories.co.uk

archive.scotsman.com

Outrageous Fortune

Bob Maslen-Jones

This is the story of a young medical student's coming-of-age. After answering the call-to-arms, the reader learns of the author's development from a young, ambitious army officer, through his training in the Indian Army and commissions in Burma and Korea until his sudden resignation 14 years later.

An expert storyteller, Bob relates numerous experiences from overseas including his stirring narrative of 18 months in the Korean Sami-ch'on Valley. An absorbing and inspiring story of great human interest.

'[Outrageous Fortune] *is a candid memoir, the author clearly shows the attitudes of the pre-war Indian Army officers and gives a useful insight into the Indian soldiers serving with the Guides.'* The Military Historical Society

ISBN 1-904445-23-3 • 240 × 170 mm • 256 pages
liberally illustrated • softback • £16.99

The Enigmatic Sailor,
Memoirs of a Seagoing Intelligence Officer

Sir Alan Peacock, DSC

Foreword by Libby Purves
The part played by code-cracking in World War II has at last been dramatically revealed in a popular film and countless broadcasts and has also inspired several accounts by code-crackers.

Much less well-known is how code-cracking was used in operational situations. Now the 'Silent Service' at last speaks through the voice of a young and inexperienced naval officer whose rites of passage to manhood required him to act as a seagoing eavesdropper, a role calling not only for quick intelligence but also for facing up to excitement and danger. He was awarded the Distinguished Service Cross for his efforts.

His story is interlarded with graphic accounts of life on the lower deck, being torpedoed in a Channel action, and how to contribute to intelligence information that was required to foil enemy attacks on Russian convoys whilst facing atrocious weather conditions.

'*This uncommonly reflective memoir provides a unique insight into the world of "Headache", the tactical equivalent of the well-known Enigma … A significant addition to the literature of the Second World War,* The Enigmatic Sailor *combines insight with eloquence'*. Times Literary Supplement

ISBN 1-904445-09-8 • 240 × 170 mm • 144 pages
illustrated with maps and photographs • softback • £14.95

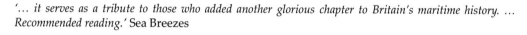
Island Base: Ascension Island in the Falklands War

Captain Bob McQueen

Foreword by **First Sea Lord Admiral Sir Alan West**

The previously untold story of how Ascension Island was crucial to the success of
British operations during the Falklands War. The book spans the duration of the
Falklands War and tells how a facility consisting of next to nothing became the Forward Operating
Base for one of the most daring and successful displays of military force at long range in the reclamation
of British interests.

*'... it serves as a tribute to those who added another glorious chapter to Britain's maritime history. ...
Recommended reading.'* Sea Breezes

*'... An authoritative and enjoyable account of life on Ascension Island throughout the campaign. ... With
an easy-going style and dry humour, Capt. McQueen gives lively descriptions of constantly hectic life.'*
Airforces Monthly

ISBN 1-904445-18-7 • 240 × 170 mm • 144 pages
liberally illustrated softback • £15.95

Not Really What You'd Call a War

Norman Hampson

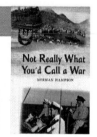

Created from the author's diaries, recollections and letters home, this book conveys
a vivid impression of how it felt to be a British Naval Liaison Officer in a Free
French sloop during WWII. Roughly half of the book deals with the very special
atmosphere in southern France immediately after its liberation in August, 1944. A
gently humorous and enjoyable read.

*'His first-hand observations and his sense of "history from below decks" provide a welcome counterweight to
conventional accounts'.* Journal of Military History

*'... a captivating portrait of the culture clash between a first-year undergraduate and a vast, historic and
uncomprehending organization. ... This is a book for those who like their wars punctuated by insight, irony
and a good measure of Catch-22'.* Times Literary Supplement

ISBN 1-870325-38-9 • 240 × 170 mm • 144 pages
liberally illustrated • softback • £14.95

Whittles Publishing
Dunbeath • Caithness • Scotland •KW6 6EY • UK
Tel: +44(0)1593-731 333; Fax: +44(0)1593-731 400;
e-mail: info@whittlespublishing.com
www.whittlespublishing.com